PAIRED PASSAGES

Grade 4

Credits
Content Editor: Pamela Walker McKenzie
Copy Editor: Julie B. Killian

Visit *carsondellosa.com* for correlations to Common Core, state, national, and Canadian provincial standards.

Carson-Dellosa Publishing, LLC
PO Box 35665
Greensboro, NC 27425 USA
carsondellosa.com

ISBN 978-1-4838-3068-1
04-282171151

Table of Contents

Introduction

As students sharpen their reading comprehension skills, they become better readers. Improving these skills has never been more important as teachers struggle to meet the rigorous college- and career-ready expectations of today's educational standards.

This book offers pairings of high-interest fiction and nonfiction passages that will appeal to even the most reluctant readers. The passages have grade-level readability. Follow-up pages promote specific questioning based on evidence from the passages.

Throughout the book, students are encouraged to practice close reading, focusing on details to make inferences from each passage separately and then as a set. The text-dependent questions and activities that follow the passages encourage students to synthesize the information they have read, leading to deeper comprehension.

How to Use This Book

Three types of pairings divide this book: fiction with nonfiction, nonfiction with nonfiction, and fiction with fiction. The book is broken down further into 22 sets of paired passages that are combined with follow-up questions and activities. Each reading passage is labeled Fiction or Nonfiction.

The passages in this book may be used in any order but should be completed as four-page sets so that students read the passages in the correct pairs. The pairs of passages have been carefully chosen and each pair has topics or elements in common.

Two pages of questions and activities follow each pair of passages to support student comprehension. The questions and activities are based on evidence that students can find in the texts. No further research is required. Students will answer a set of questions that enable comprehension of each of the two passages. The questions range in format and include true/false, multiple choice, and short answer. The final questions or activities ask students to compare and contrast details or elements from the two passages.

Assessment Rubric

Use this rubric as a guide for assessing students' work. It can also be offered to students to help them check their work or as a tool to show your scoring.

4	_____ Independently reads and comprehends grade-level texts _____ Easily compares and contrasts authors' purposes _____ Uses higher-order thinking skills to link common themes or ideas _____ References both passages when comparing and contrasting _____ Uses vivid dialogue where appropriate _____ Skillfully summarizes reading based on textual evidence
3	_____ Needs little support for comprehension of grade-level texts _____ Notes some comparisons of authors' purposes _____ Infers broad common themes or ideas _____ Connects key ideas and general themes of both passages _____ Uses textual evidence to summarize reading with some support
2	_____ Needs some support for comprehension of grade-level texts _____ Understands overt similarities in authors' purposes _____ Links stated or obvious common themes or ideas _____ Compares and contrasts both passages with support _____ Summarizes reading based on textual evidence with difficulty
1	_____ Reads and comprehends grade-level text with assistance _____ Cannot compare or contrast authors' purposes _____ Has difficulty linking common themes or ideas _____ Cannot connect the information from both passages _____ Is unable to use textual evidence to summarize reading

Old Frog's Tail

Adapted from "Why Grandfather Frog Has No Tail" by Thornton W. Burgess

One day, Old Frog sat near the pond in a patch of brown cattails. "*Gaaaarumph!*" he croaked. A bright peacock strolled over and stood near the lumpy brown frog, spreading his feathers and letting the brilliant colors catch the sunlight.

"Have you ever seen a more dazzling sight?" Peacock boasted.

"I once had a tail that was every bit as beautiful," Old Frog said. "In fact, all frogs had bright, sweeping tails. We sat by the pond and swished our tails this way and that. I boasted that my tail was lovelier than any frog's tail in the land!"

Peacock was astounded! Did this lumpy frog once have a tail as fine-looking as his own? "Where is your tail now?" the curious bird asked.

"I boasted too often," Old Frog lamented. "Mother Nature felt that our colorful tails had caused frogs to become lazy and vain. Over time, our tails grew smaller until they finally disappeared."

"That's terrible!" Peacock exclaimed.

Old Frog nodded. "We are each left with a reminder. Now, every frog begins life in a pond with a small gray tail. As soon as we hatch, we must use those tails to swim away from hungry creatures. Gradually, our tails disappear, and we grow legs. Finally, we crawl onto the pond bank. As we sit by the pond and see our reflections, we think about the tails we lost."

Peacock looked at the water, admiring the splendor of his colorful tail. But, this time he did not say a word.

Tadpole to Frog

A frog sits on the sunny bank of a pond. This frog's life has seen many changes. This frog has faced many dangers too. Let's look at a frog's journey from tadpole to frog.

A frog begins life as a tiny egg in the water. It floats in a jelly-like cluster of hundreds of other eggs. Within a few days, the eggs hatch. Now, tiny tadpoles swim for their lives! A pond is home to many different kinds of animals that love to eat the tadpoles. Out of the hundreds of tadpoles that hatch, only a few survive to adulthood.

If a tadpole is able to escape its predators long enough, it begins to change. This change is called **metamorphosis**. It is an important step in the life cycle of a frog. It begins when tiny little legs begin to grow along either side of the tadpole. The tadpole's head begins to change too, showing some features of the frog that it will become. While this is taking place, the tadpole's tail becomes smaller and smaller. Finally, its tail disappears.

Changes are taking place inside the tadpole too. As its gills begin to disappear, the tadpole develops lungs that will allow it to breathe once it leaves the water as a frog. When the metamorphosis is complete, the frog climbs out of the water and onto land. There it will stay until it is time to lay eggs. Then, the cycle will begin again.

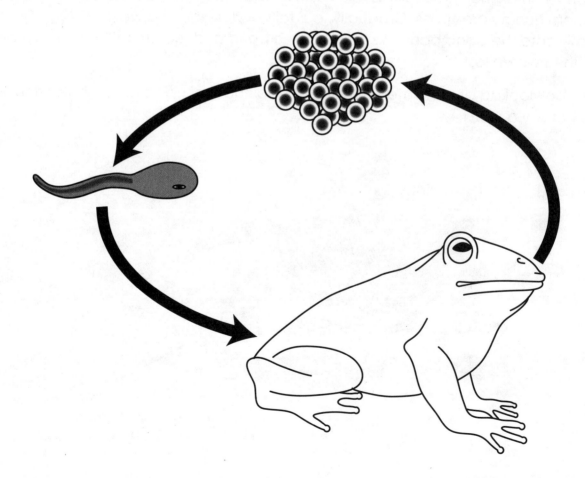

Name _____

Answer the questions.

1. What was the author's purpose in writing "Old Frog's Tail"?

   A. to explain the life cycle of a frog

   B. to compare a frog to a peacock

   C. to teach a lesson about boasting

   D. to show ways that frogs have changed over time

2. According to "Old Frog's Tail," why did Mother Nature take away the tails of frogs?

   A. The frogs needed a reminder of what they once had.

   B. The frogs were becoming lazy and vain.

   C. The peacocks' tails were more beautiful.

   D. The frogs had forgotten how to swim.

3. What is the main idea of "Tadpole to Frog"?

   A. A frog lays hundreds of eggs in the water.

   B. A frog changes as part of its life cycle.

   C. Lungs help frogs breathe out of the water.

   D. It is fun to watch a tadpole change into a frog.

4. According to "Tadpole to Frog," what danger do tadpoles face?

   A. eggs that hatch too early

   B. changes to the tadpoles' tails

   C. gills that disappear

   D. predators that eat tadpoles

5. What is the moral, or lesson, of "Old Frog's Tail"?

   _____

   _____

6. What does the word **metamorphosis** mean as it is used in "Tadpole to Frog"?

   _____

   _____

Name _____

7. Complete the chart to tell how Old Frog changed in "Old Frog's Tail." Then, tell what you learned in "Tadpole to Frog" about the way all frogs change.

	At first, . . .	Then, . . .	Finally, . . .
How Old Frog changed			
How all frogs change			

8. What do the two passages have in common?

_____

_____

_____

_____

9. How are the two passages different?

_____

_____

_____

_____

8

A Sleeping Beast

Long ago lived a ruler named Hekla who became so evil that his subjects chased him into the sea. He swam as long as he could, but soon exhaustion overtook him. A whale took pity on the man and carried him on his back. After many days, they arrived at a beautiful island.

The people on the island told the weak man that he was fortunate. "We call our home Iceland," they said. "This is a land of ice, but our hearts are warm. We will help you get healthy again." And, that is just what they did.

Soon, Hekla was strong enough to explore the island. People accepted him warmly, but the darkness in Hekla's heart had never left. He began demanding that people call him their ruler. He claimed to know what was best for the island.

"We do not need a ruler," the people reasoned. "Our only rule is to be kind to each other." Hekla laughed at them. He took half the fish they brought from the sea for himself. He built a prison for anyone who disobeyed him.

One day, the people heard a menacing rumble. Suddenly, a mountaintop exploded in fire. A great volcano had erupted! Had Hekla angered the sleeping beast? The people pleaded with him to show kindness. But Hekla, fearful of the volcano, ran into the sea. Immediately, the volcano became silent.

Peace returned, but from then on, the people called the volcano Hekla. It was a reminder of the importance of always showing kindness.

Fire and Ice

Between North America and Europe lies an island. The island is just below the Arctic Circle. Much of the land is covered in glaciers, or large sheets of ice and snow. But, this tiny nation was born from fire, not ice. This land is called Iceland.

More than 20 million years ago, volcanoes spewed lava from the seafloor. The cooling lava grew until it rose above sea level, creating the island. Iceland has both mountain peaks and desert land. Inlets, carved by glaciers, ring the coast. Small pools of water, heated by the rocks below, emit steam.

Just over 300,000 people live in Iceland. Most people live near the cities on the coast. Many people in Iceland enjoy nature. They appreciate the beauty of the land. Hiking and ice climbing are two ways the people have fun outdoors. But, they are also aware that they live near active volcanoes.

In 2010, a volcano erupted after being dormant for almost 200 years. This volcano in southern Iceland blasted ash miles into the air. Hot lava poured down the side of the mountain. As ash fell, the sky became dark. Dense ash clouds caused airlines to cancel flights. The ash could damage airplane engines. The danger was too great.

Iceland is home to both icebergs and hot springs. The island has blue lagoons and black sand. Iceland is a land of extremes. It has snowy mountains and fiery volcanoes. Iceland has earned its nickname, the Land of Fire and Ice.

Name _____

Answer the questions.

1. Is "A Sleeping Beast" fiction or nonfiction? Explain your answer.

_____

_____

2. Is "Fire and Ice" fiction or nonfiction? Explain your answer.

_____

_____

3. What is the central message of "Fire and Ice"?

   A. The people of Iceland enjoy outdoor activities.

   B. Volcanoes in Iceland are causing many problems.

   C. Iceland is a place known for having both ice and volcanoes.

   D. Iceland was formed millions of years ago from volcanoes.

4. Which sentence best summarizes the first paragraph of "A Sleeping Beast"?

   A. Hekla did not care for his subjects, and he made them angry.

   B. A whale rescued a ruler who had been kind to whales.

   C. A ruler who could not swim well became too exhausted to continue.

   D. After being chased into the sea, an evil ruler was taken to an island by a whale.

5. Which phrase from "Fire and Ice" helps the reader understand inlets?

   A. carved by glaciers   **B.** ring the coast

   C. small pools of water   **D.** desert land

6. Write **true** or **false**. Then, explain your answer.

   _____ According to "Fire and Ice," the volcano eruption in 2010 was not a surprise because many smaller eruptions had occurred.

   _____

   _____

Name _____

7. Complete the chart to tell about the author's purpose and main idea in each passage.

	A Sleeping Beast	Fire and Ice
Author's Purpose		
Main Idea		

8. What can you learn about Iceland in each passage? How is the information in the two passages different?

_____

_____

_____

_____

_____

_____

_____

_____

_____

_____

Anna's New Home

Dear Anna,

Do you like New York City? What is your new home like? Do you have a big backyard with a swing like your old Greenville home? I miss you every day. Please write soon!

Your friend,

Marisa

Dear Marisa,

I miss you too! I miss Greenville, but I also like my new home here in the city. Our apartment building has 58 floors. We are on the 55th floor.

My new home is a busy place filled with a lot of people and all kinds of activities. Hundreds of families live here! I think this building has everything anyone could ever need. I do not have a backyard, but our building has an exercise gym that is all the way up on the 58th floor!

On the fourth floor, a daycare is open for the children who live in the building. That's where my mom works, taking care of the babies in the nursery.

Two of my favorite places are on the first floor near the lobby. One is a bakery that makes fresh bread every day in many different shapes. The other is a flower shop that is filled with **an explosion of colorful blooms**. Mrs. Ling owns the shop, and she knows absolutely everything about flowers!

Maybe you can visit soon, and I will show you my new home!

Your friend,

Anna

The Busy Hive

Have you ever heard anyone say, "as busy as a bee"? Look inside a honeybee hive, and you will see just how busy bees can be. A honeybee hive buzzes with all the activities the bees need to survive.

Honeybees make their hives from a wax that they secrete from their bodies. The wax needs heat to make it soft enough to shape. Bees beat their wings to heat the air. They form the warmed wax into small six-sided cells that are attached to each other. A sheet of these cells is called a comb.

A typical hive contains about 100,000 cells. The cells support the weight of the bees, as well as all of the honey that fills the combs. About 30,000 bees make up a honeybee **colony**. Bees can produce as much as 40 pounds of honey in a season.

Some of the cells in a hive are used for food storage. Bees visit nearby flowers and then return with pollen. The bees feed some of the pollen to the young bees to help them grow. The bees also return with the sweet nectar from flowers. Back at the hive, the busy bees turn the nectar into honey. When winter comes, honeybees will have plenty of food stored in the hive!

The hive is also a nursery. Special workers called nurse bees care for young, newly hatched bees. When the young bees are old enough, they leave the nursery and join the other bees in the busy hive that is their home!

Name _____

Answer the questions.

1. What was the author's purpose in writing "The Busy Hive"?

    A. to tell about the different activities that take place in a hive

    B. to explain how bees gather pollen and nectar

    C. to entertain readers with a story about honeybees

    D. to teach a lesson about the importance of staying busy

2. What does the phrase **an explosion of colorful blooms** mean in "Anna's New Home"?

    A. The flowers in the shop were on fire.

    B. Flower blooms were all over the floor.

    C. The shop had a variety of brightly colored flowers in it.

    D. The flowers were all one color.

3. Why do you think Anna tells Marisa about her two favorite places in the building?

    A. Marisa would like to live near a bakery and flower shop.

    B. Marisa has never seen an apartment building before.

    C. Anna wants Marisa to know the reasons she likes her new home.

    D. Anna hopes that Marisa will visit her soon.

4. Write **true** or **false**.

    _____ Bees create hives using a type of wax that they form into cells.

5. Bees gather _____ from flowers and then change it into honey.

6. Anna moved from _____ to New York City.

7. What does the word **colony** mean as it is used in "The Busy Hive"?

    _____

    _____

Name _____

8. Complete the graphic organizer to compare a honeybee hive to the apartment building described in "Anna's New Home." Tell what is the same and what is different about each type of home.

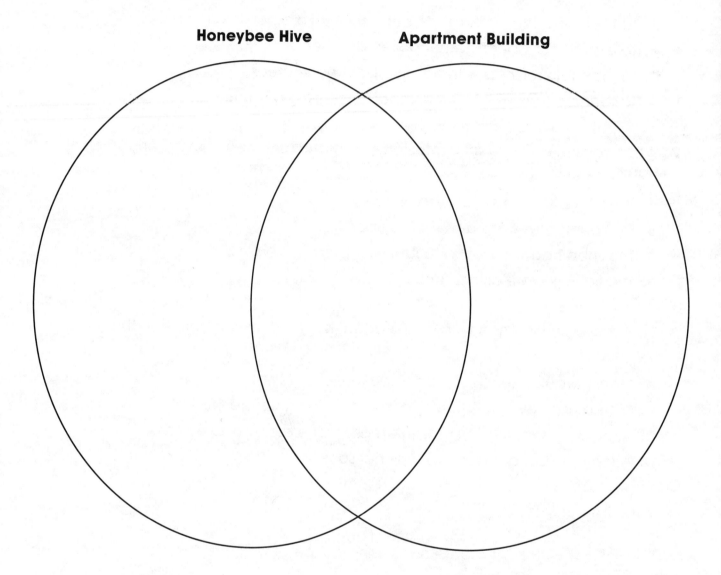

Honeybee Hive   **Apartment Building**

9. Write a paragraph that describes a place or item you have seen that is another kind of home similar to a honeybee hive or Anna's apartment building.

_____

_____

_____

_____

A Box and a Can

"Benji Becker, I know you don't want to,

but it's time to clean your room!"

Benji Becker shook his head,

filled with sadness and gloom.

"Here is a box for your toys and

a can for your junk.

Everything must have a place,

even this remote-controlled skunk."

Benji Becker picked up T. rex

and dropped him in the box.

In went a rubbery black-and-white shark,

In went five mismatched socks.

Into the box went some old chewing gum,

In went three wooden trains.

Into the box went hundreds of marbles,

In went some broken chains.

"Benji Becker, your box is full,

but nothing is in the can!"

Benji Becker smiled and said,

"I know! That was my plan!"

Space Junk

Someone needs to clean up Earth's neighborhood! Space is littered with space junk. This man-made material is no longer useful, but it still orbits Earth. And, it is a growing problem.

The size of space junk varies. Some pieces are no bigger than bugs. Other pieces can be as large as trucks! Some space junk is made up of old satellites and rockets that have stopped working. These larger pieces can collide and break apart. This makes even more space junk. The National Aeronautics and Space Administration (NASA) reports that space junk is made up of millions of pieces of plastic, metal, and glass. Even a tool bag was left behind up there!

Is space junk a real problem? Most experts believe that it is. The junk whirls around our planet at a staggering speed. At 17,000 miles (27,360 km) an hour, even a small piece can cause problems. Space junk has damaged more than 80 space shuttle windows over the years. A chain reaction of space junk collisions could destroy satellites that we use to communicate and to predict weather.

Who should clean up the mess in space? How can it be cleaned up? How can it be prevented? Experts from many countries are now working together to answer these questions. Space junk is not a problem that will go away on its own.

Name _____

Answer the questions.

1. Is "A Box and a Can" fiction or nonfiction? Explain your answer.

_____

_____

2. What genre is "A Box and a Can"? How do you know?

_____

_____

3. Is "Space Junk" fiction or nonfiction? Explain your answer.

_____

_____

4. What genre is "Space Junk"? How do you know?

_____

_____

5. Why do you think Benji said, "I know! That was my plan!" at the end of the poem?

    A. His mom was happy that he cleaned his room.

    B. He did not want to throw anything away.

    C. He could not find his T. rex.

    D. He did not know what to put in the can.

6. Which statement best expresses the author's opinion in "Space Junk"?

    A. Space junk is a problem, and it needs to be cleaned up.

    B. Space junk is not a very big problem.

    C. NASA should clean up the space junk.

    D. Space junk has damaged many space shuttle windows.

Name _____

7. Cleaning up junk was a central idea in the poem "A Box and a Can" and in the article "Space Junk." Complete the chart to compare the different ideas and details about junk in each passage.

	A Box and a Can	**Space Junk**
Kinds of Junk		
Why is junk a problem?		
What is the solution?		

8. What do the two passages have in common?

_____

_____

_____

_____

9. How are the two passages different?

_____

_____

_____

_____

An Important Day

November 1, 1870

Dear Diary,

Father comes home today! Mother is planning a rather large celebration to welcome him. I have missed him so much! Mother reminds me daily, "The work your father is doing will long be remembered."

Father has been part of an expedition to explore land In the Yellowstone Plateau, which is out west. He has been making maps to show what the land is like. Father says that the place must be seen to be believed. He describes hot springs in which steam rolls from the surface. He sent me a sketch of a fountain of water that shoots out of the ground many times a day! Father says that this natural feature is called a geyser. The explorers have given it the name Old Faithful. He laughs that it is more predictable than train service here in Boston!

Some of the men who were with Father wrote reports about the wildlife in the area. Others examined and took samples of the plant life. They made many sketches to record what the explorers discovered on their trip.

Father says that they will present the reports with the sketches and his maps to President Grant. They hope that the president will set aside this land so that it may be preserved. Father feels that it should be a national park. If it is preserved, everyone can visit it and see its wonders.

I must go now. Mother is calling me to help her make a cake for Father!

Ever yours,

Nora

Geysers

Few sights in nature are more thrilling than a geyser erupting. Boiling water and steam shoot out of the ground at amazing speeds. The English word *geyser* is borrowed from the Icelandic word *geysir*, which means "to gush." And, that is what a geyser does. It gushes gallons of hot water from the ground. The water and steam shoot skyward!

Geysers are found in places with a lot of volcanic activity. Think of a geyser as a vent in the earth's surface. Rain and snow seep into the cracks. Deep in the earth, the water reaches magma, or hot liquid rock. The water is heated and begins to boil. When enough pressure builds, the geyser erupts. A column of hot water shoots out of the vent and into the sky.

Only a few countries have active geysers. The United States, Russia, and Iceland are three of those places. All three have the kind of volcanic activity that forms geysers. In the United States, Yellowstone National Park is the place to see geysers. In fact, it has more geysers than any other place on Earth.

Old Faithful is the best-known geyser in Yellowstone National Park. Its name fits. Old Faithful is an easy geyser to predict. On average, the geyser erupts about once per hour. The soaring water can reach an amazing 180 feet (55 m) high. Tourists are thrilled to see Old Faithful erupt. Cheers often go up along with the water and steam!

Name _____

Answer the questions.

I. According to "An Important Day," why is Father's work important?

    A. His work could lead to preserving the land as a national park.

    B. No one had ever seen geysers before.

    C. Father will get to meet President Grant one day.

    D. The trip was exciting and dangerous.

2. In "Geysers," why does the author include the Icelandic word *geysir*?

    A. to describe the vent of a geyser

    B. to explain why geysers gush water

    C. to explain where the word *geyser* comes from

    D. to show that most geysers are in Iceland

3. What can you learn from both passages about the name "Old Faithful"?

    A. The men who explored the land named the geyser.

    B. It is called Old Faithful because it is predictable.

    C. A sign states that its name is Old Faithful.

    D. It erupts about once per hour.

4. According to "Geysers," what must be present for geysers to form?

    A. vents   **B.** steam

    C. rain and snow   **D.** volcanic activity

5. What work did Nora's father and the other men do on their expedition?

    _____

    _____

6. What role does magma play in the eruption of a geyser?

    _____

    _____

Name _____

7. What can you learn about Yellowstone National Park from both passages? Use details from the diary entry and the article to support your answer.

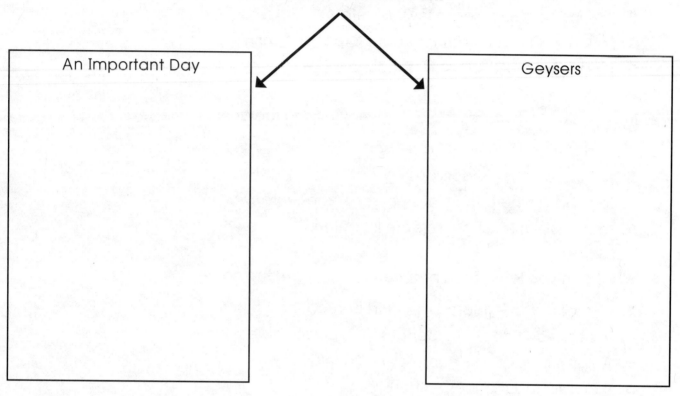

Yellowstone National Park

An Important Day

Geysers

8. Write a summary about what you learned about Yellowstone National Park using information from each passage.

_____

_____

_____

_____

_____

_____

_____

_____

_____

One Golden Egg

Long ago, a poor farmer and his wife owned one goose that laid one egg each day. They would have starved if not for that goose.

One morning when the farmer collected the egg, he was surprised to find a glittery egg of pure gold. At first, he was disappointed. How could they live on this egg! They needed food!

His wife pointed out that the goose had given them a wonderful gift, because now they could buy a cow and a sheep. They would have milk and cheese to eat and wool to make clothing. "We will never be poor again with a sheep and a cow!" she explained.

"We will never be poor again," the farmer said, "because we have a goose that lays golden eggs."

In the village, the farmer traded the egg for a basket of food and silk clothing, while his wife shook her head in disappointment.

The next morning, the farmer dreamed of what he would buy with the next golden egg. Perhaps a fine horse, he thought, for he was certain he would look quite dashing riding a mighty steed.

But, the nest contained only one ordinary egg that morning. "Where is my golden egg?" he bellowed.

The farmer's words terrified the goose. She darted from her nest, flew into the sky, and was never seen again.

Soon, the basket of food was empty, and the silk clothing was tattered. With the goose gone, the farmer and his wife were poorer than they had ever been.

Gold Rush

The year was 1848. James Marshall was building a sawmill near the American River in what is now California. Marshall looked down at the water and spotted something glittery. He reached in and retrieved several shiny rocks. He wondered if the rocks were fool's gold. Those worthless rocks looked like gold and had fooled many. After a closer look, Marshall knew that this was the real thing. He took the gold to his employer, John Sutter.

The two men became partners. They tried to keep the discovery a secret. But, news that gold had been found at Sutter's Mill spread and was all anyone talked about. By 1849, people poured into the area. Everyone hoped to strike it rich. The gold rush had begun.

Between 1849 and 1858, hundreds of thousands of people rushed to California. The risks were great for these prospectors. Often, the miners had given up all they owned for a chance at finding gold. In some cases, the risk was worth it. Some people found gold and became rich. But, many others did not. A few found other ways to make money. They provided goods and services to the crowds of miners flooding the camps.

Neither James Marshall nor John Sutter ever became wealthy. The men had no legal claim to the land where they found gold. As time passed, fewer prospectors found gold. People began leaving the camps to go home. Others chose to stay. Many former mining camps are now the towns and cities in California.

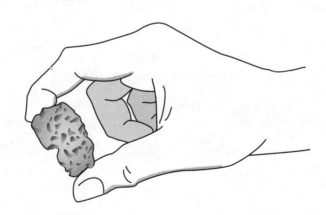

Name _____

Answer the questions.

I. Is "One Golden Egg" fiction or nonfiction? Explain your answer.

_____

_____

2. What genre is "One Golden Egg"? How do you know?

_____

_____

3. Is "Gold Rush" fiction or nonfiction? Explain your answer.

_____

_____

4. What genre is "Gold Rush"? How do you know?

_____

_____

5. The words _____ in the sixth paragraph of "One Golden Egg" mean the same as "a fine horse."

6. Write **true** or **false**. Then, explain your answer.

_____ In "One Golden Egg," the farmer's wife did not agree with her husband about what they should do with the egg.

_____

_____

_____ According to "Gold Rush," the only people who got rich were the prospectors who found gold.

_____

_____

Name _____

7. Complete the chart to tell about cause and effect in each passage.

One Golden Egg

Cause	Effect
A.	A. The farmer and his wife bought food and clothing.
B. The farmer scared the goose.	B.
C. The farmer and his wife no longer had the goose.	C.

Gold Rush

Cause	Effect
A. James Marshall built a sawmill on the river.	A.
B.	B. People rushed into the area to find gold.
C.	C. Some people left the mining camps.

8. How is gold and wealth a central message in each passage?

_____

_____

_____

_____

_____

_____

_____

John Henry and His Sledgehammer

When John Henry was a baby, he was not so different from anyone else. He smiled, cried, and crawled around on the floor. He giggled, burped, and threw the occasional fit. But, all of that changed one day when he happened upon a sledgehammer and a pile of rocks.

Four-year-old John Henry lifted the sledgehammer and brought it down with a mighty crash on a rock bigger than a horse. Nothing was left but a pile of dust.

When John Henry was old enough, he took a job with the new railroad being built through the mountains. All day, he hammered steel spikes and laid heavy railroad ties. When the workers came upon a big rock, John Henry smashed it to bits so that the railroad could move on.

One day, a stranger arrived with a drilling machine. He claimed that his machine could do more work than John Henry and be faster too! John Henry laughed and pointed to a wall of rock. "Let's see who can get through that!" he challenged.

The steam drill and John Henry got to work. Machine and man worked side by side in dust so thick that it was hard to see who was winning. But, the winner was clear by the following day.

John Henry, smiling, held his hammer high. He had broken through the rock wall! Next to him was the steam drill, smoking, sputtering, and finally quitting altogether in a pitiful whimper.

Some people say that John Henry never really left the tunnel he helped to carve out of the mountain. They say that John Henry's image is engraved on a big rock in that tunnel. Legend has it that sometimes you can even hear the sound of a pair of sledgehammers still at work.

A Time of Great Change

In the early 1800s, a shift began to take place in the world. For the next 100 years, the way people made things changed. The way people traveled changed. The way people communicated changed. This was the time of the Industrial Revolution. It was a time of great change.

Before these changes, people made things with their hands. People wove cloth from wool, cotton, and silk and sewed the cloth into clothing. The sewing machine changed that. Factories opened with sewing machines that helped people make clothing. Sewing with machines was much faster than sewing by hand.

Land travel once meant going by horse, buggy, or wagon. Thanks to the steam engine, train travel became possible. Steam drills blasted through rock as men laid track for the new trains. A steam drill could do the work of dozens of men using sledgehammers.

Steam improved water travel too. Sailing ships needed wind for power. Canoes and rafts traveled downstream easily. But, upstream travel was more difficult. The steam engine easily powered a riverboat upstream. Over land and water, people and goods moved across the country at record speeds.

This progress also changed the way people communicated. Steamboats and trains moved mail. Letters that had taken a month to arrive, now took only days. The telegraph made communication even faster.

The years of the Industrial Revolution changed America. People saw their lives improve in some ways. But, some felt the changes were not good. That is a debate that still goes on today.

Name _____

Answer the questions.

1. What is the first clue in "John Henry and His Sledgehammer" that the story is a tall tale?

   A. He crawled on the floor.

   B. He crushed a huge rock with a sledgehammer.

   C. He took a job with the railroad.

   D. He challenged the steam drill to a contest.

2. According to "A Time of Great Change," what did the sewing machine change?

   A. the way cloth was woven   **B.** how factories were built

   C. how fast clothing could be made   **D.** how people communicated

3. In "John Henry and His Sledgehammer," what is the likely reason that John Henry challenged the steam drill to a contest?

   A. He was certain that he was stronger and faster than the machine.

   B. He wanted to show off his strength.

   C. The other workers wanted him to do it.

   D. He did not like the stranger with the steam drill.

4. What are some ways that steam power changed travel?

   _____

   _____

5. How did John Henry's strength help in building the railroad?

   _____

   _____

6. "John Henry and His Sledgehammer" is a tall tale that uses exaggeration. Would a real person and a sledgehammer be able to win a contest against a steam drill? Use facts from "A Time of Great Change" to support your answer.

   _____

   _____

Name _____

7. Complete the chart to organize what you learned from both passages.

	John Henry and His Sledgehammer	**A Time of Great Change**
Main Idea		
Three Details		
Summary		

8. What are some things that both passages tell about people and their work?

_____

_____

_____

_____

_____

_____

_____

A Long Journey

My grandson wants me to tell the story about how I came to America. He gave me this beautiful journal and asked me to write my story. I love my grandson very much, so if he wants me to write my story, I will do that.

I have lived many years in this beautiful country, but I was not born here. It was a long journey that took me from Italy to the shores of America. I was only a boy of seven. My father had died the year before, and we were very poor. My mother wanted us to have a better life. She had cousins in America who began sending letters, pleading with us to join them.

We began to save our money until we had enough for the trip. Our accommodations were in **steerage** because we could not afford tickets that provided a private cabin. Steerage was just below the main deck, and it was filled with sleeping bunks. It contained little fresh air. We were on the ship for 12 days.

Then came our final morning. A feeling of excitement was on board. We would arrive soon! Everyone cheered when the Statue of Liberty became visible. She seemed to be holding out her torch just for us! What a kind face this lady had. And, she was so tall! I told my mother that America must be a land of giants. Mama laughed and cried too, but she cried only tears of joy!

Armando Marino

A Birthday Gift

The Statue of Liberty stands in New York Harbor. Lady Liberty, as she is often called, holds her torch high. This statue is a symbol of freedom. She has welcomed immigrants to the United States since 1886.

The statue was a gift to America for its 100th birthday. The idea came from a dinner party in Paris, France. The guests discussed ways that they could honor the United States. The French people felt a bond with Americans. Both nations shared a belief in freedom.

One guest was a sculptor. He suggested a statue of a woman holding a torch. She would represent freedom. Many agreed that this would be an ideal gift. The sculptor's name was Frédéric-Auguste Bartholdi.

Bartholdi began to make sketches. Then, he toured the United States. He wanted to find the perfect place for the statue. He saw a small island in New York Harbor. The sculptor could imagine the statue's torch shining across the water. The island was just right.

Back in France, Bartholdi hired a crew. They got to work. Nine years later, they finished the statue. It was time to send the gift to America. But, first they had to take it apart. Bartholdi sent 350 pieces to New York City. Then, it was put back together.

The statue was unveiled on October 28, 1886. More than one million people came to cheer and see the veil removed. Today, about four million people visit the statue each year. Lady Liberty is an enduring symbol of freedom and friendship.

Name _____

Answer the questions.

1. Why did Armando's grandson give him a journal?

    A. It was a nice birthday gift for his grandfather.

    B. He wanted Armando to write about coming to America.

    C. Armando had always wanted a journal.

    D. He liked to hear his grandfather's stories.

2. What is the main reason that Armando and his mother left Italy?

    A. to see the Statue of Liberty   B. to visit their family

    C. to have an exciting adventure   D. to have opportunities for a better life

3. What special bond did the French and Americans have?

    A. They shared a birthday.

    B. Both countries liked statues.

    C. Freedom was important to both countries.

    D. Bartholdi was French but enjoyed visiting America.

4. What is the main reason that Bartholdi chose the island in New York Harbor for the statue?

    A. The island was affordable.

    B. He needed a large place to put the statue.

    C. The people in New York wanted the statue there.

    D. He was able to picture what the statue would look like there.

5. What does the word **steerage** mean as it is used in "A Long Journey"?

    _____

    _____

6. What did the author of "A Birthday Gift" mean by saying that the statue was "an ideal gift"?

    _____

    _____

Name _____

7. Complete the chart to tell what you learned about the Statue of Liberty. Include information and details from both passages.

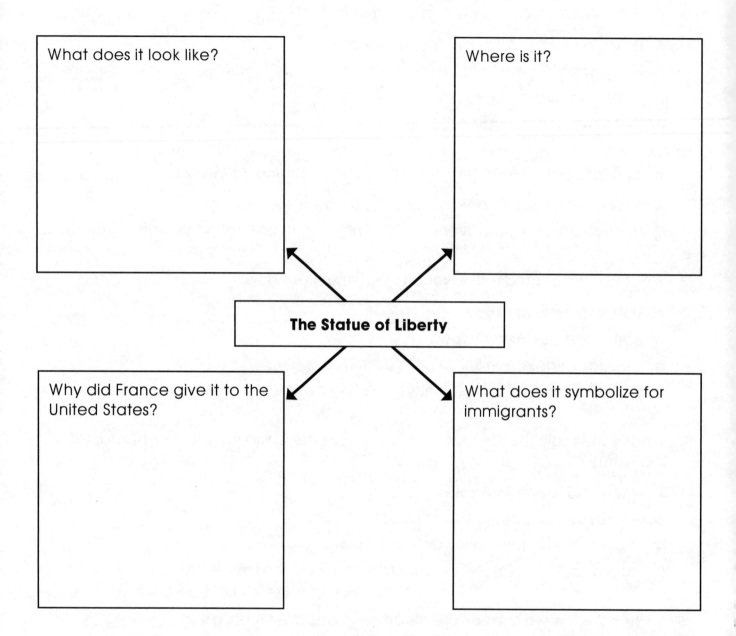

What does it look like?

Where is it?

The Statue of Liberty

Why did France give it to the United States?

What does it symbolize for immigrants?

8. What if Bartholdi, the sculptor who made the Statue of Liberty, could have read Armando's journal entry? How do you think Bartholdi would have felt? Use details from both passages to help you answer the questions.

_____

_____

_____

White House Pets

George Washington owned a dog named Madame Moose. Alice Roosevelt, daughter of Theodore Roosevelt, had a garter snake named Emily Spinach. John Quincy Adams once received an alligator as a gift. For a time, this toothy pet lived in a White House bathtub!

The White House is home to the United States president and the president's family. It is also home to the family's pets. Many cats, dogs, and birds have lived in the White House. Warren Harding's family once held a birthday party for their dog, Laddie. Guests included other dogs. These guests enjoyed a tasty dog biscuit cake!

Some pets lived outside. Woodrow Wilson found a smart way to keep the lawn trimmed. Sheep nibbled the grass. Cows, horses, and goats have also lived on the White House lawn. When Theodore Roosevelt's son Archie was ill, his father wanted to cheer him up. He put Archie's pony on the elevator and brought him to his room.

Tad, a son of Abraham Lincoln, owned a turkey named Jack. As time for a holiday feast approached, Tad asked his father to spare his pet's life. Tad did not want Jack to become dinner. His father agreed and signed an official pardon. Tad saved Jack! The tradition continues. Each year, the current president pardons a turkey.

Some pets, such as cats and dogs, are typical. Snakes and alligators are more unusual. For many people, pets are just part of the family, even when that family lives in the White House!

The Problem with Exotic Pets

Do you have a pet? Do your friends have pets? More than half of the homes in the United States have at least one pet. Dogs and cats are the most common. But, another type of pet ownership is growing. Owning exotic or wild animals has become a popular but worrisome trend.

Some of the wild animals that people keep include lions, bears, tigers, monkeys, and pythons. Each year, more wild animal attacks are reported. The owners often are not trained to care for these animals. Without proper care, the animals can suffer and die in captivity. Some are abandoned. These animals then become threats to anyone who happens to find them.

Another danger from owning an exotic pet is disease. Some animal diseases can be spread to humans. In 2003, a region of the United States experienced an outbreak of a disease called monkeypox. Despite its name, it seems to have spread through contact with rats and prairie dogs. Dozens of people became sick. Many kinds of animal diseases are fatal to humans.

Some states now have laws that ban wild animals as pets. Yet, some people ignore these laws. Many times, states do not enforce the laws. It is important to get the word out about this problem. Owning exotic pets is not cool. Wild animals should stay in the wild.

Name _____

Answer the questions.

I. What was the author's purpose in writing "White House Pets"?

    A. to persuade readers to own pets

    B. to explain the reason for laws about pets

    C. to compare presidents and the kinds of pets they owned

    D. to tell about different pets owned by presidents and their families

2. According to "White House Pets," which pet helped with lawn care?

    A. monkey   **B.** dog

    C. sheep   **D.** goat

3. According to "The Problem with Exotic Pets," which pets do more people own than any others?

    A. lions and bears   **B.** cats and dogs

    C. monkeys and pythons   **D.** all exotic pets

4. Which sentence from "The Problem with Exotic Pets" best states the author's opinion?

    A. Each year, more wild animal attacks are reported.

    B. Without proper care, the animals can suffer and die in captivity.

    C. Some states have laws that ban wild animals as pets.

    D. Owning exotic pets is not cool.

Use the words in the word bank to complete the sentences.

> alligator   garter snake   turkey

5. Theodore Roosevelt's daughter owned a _____.

6. Someone once kept an _____ in a bathtub at the White House.

7. Tad Lincoln helped save the life of his pet _____.

Name _____

8. Complete the graphic organizer with facts and opinions from both passages.
You may not need to use all of the bullet points.

Facts	Opinions
•	•
•	•
•	•
•	•
•	•
•	•

9. Compare the author's purpose in writing each passage. How did each author
present the information? Use details from both passages to support your answer.

_____

_____

_____

_____

_____

_____

A Place in the World

Let's say that you are standing at a place where two paths cross. You want to walk to the market, but you cannot see the market from where you stand. To the right, the path leads through a forest. To the left, the path crosses over several hills. If you could float above where you stand, you could see the location of the market. You could see that you need to walk through the forest and turn left. A map is like the image that you see from above.

Some of the earliest maps that have been discovered date back more than 4,000 years. People in ancient Babylon made maps on clay tablets. Other examples of early mapmaking include painted maps on silk fabric from China and road maps on wooden boards from ancient Egypt.

The ancient Greeks advanced the science of cartography, or mapmaking. As they traveled, their knowledge of the world increased. Their maps began to show more detail such as the shapes of landmasses. The maps included oceans, lakes, rivers, and inlets.

Ancient maps show that people long ago were not so different from us. They wanted to better understand their world. Maps help us know where we are. They show us how to get from one place to another. Maps can even show us what we will see along the way. A map is an important tool for understanding our place in the world.

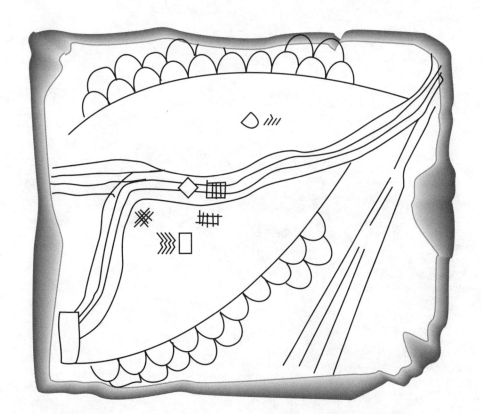

GPS: Showing You the Way

"Turn left on Oak Street," says the robotic voice on the navigation equipment in your car. "Your destination is on the right." How is it possible that you have just found your location? What technology made this possible? You can thank the global positioning system, or GPS, for helping you find your way.

GPS is made up of a set of satellites that orbit Earth. As the satellites orbit, they send a steady stream of signals. Receivers, such as the GPS in your car or on your phone, receive the signals. In fact, they receive four or more signals at any one time.

After receiving these signals, your GPS figures the distance to the satellites. It uses the data to pinpoint your exact location on Earth. As you drive down the road, your GPS receives new signals to show you where you are going. When it is time to turn left on Oak Street, your GPS will tell you.

The US military developed the first GPS for its own use. They launched the first satellite in 1978. Later, they made the system available to everyone.

Today, GPS shows us where we are. It shows us how to get where we are going. GPS has forever changed the way that we find our way around our world.

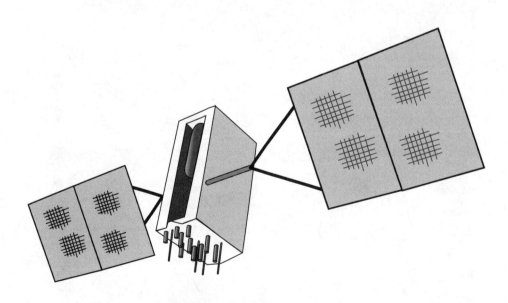

Name _____

Answer the questions.

1. What was the author's purpose in writing "A Place in the World"?

   A. to explain how to use maps

   B. to tell what early maps were like

   C. to share a funny story about mapmaking

   D. to explain the uses of different kinds of maps

2. What was the author's purpose in writing "GPS: Showing You the Way"?

   A. to describe how satellites work

   B. to tell why the military developed GPS

   C. to give information about how GPS works

   D. to persuade people to use GPS instead of maps

3. The letters GPS stand for _____ positioning system.

4. Cartography is the science of _____.

5. What are three examples of early maps according to "A Place in the World"?

   _____

   _____

6. In "GPS: Showing You the Way," the author writes, "GPS has forever changed the way that we find our way around our world." Do you agree or disagree with this statement? Explain your answer.

   _____

   _____

7. In "A Place in the World," the author states, "Ancient maps show that people long ago were not so different from us." Do you agree or disagree with this statement? Explain your answer.

   _____

   _____

Name _____

8. Compare maps from long ago with the GPS technology that we use today. Use details from both passages to tell what is the same and what is different about each.

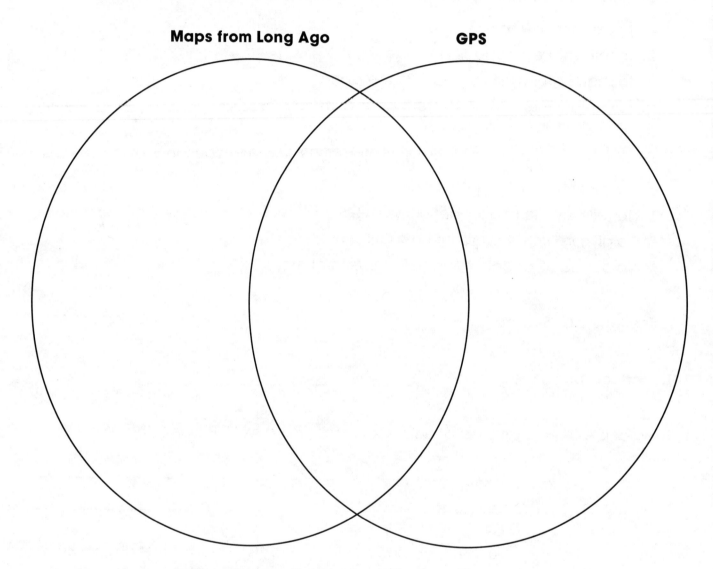

Maps from Long Ago   **GPS**

9. Write a brief conversation you might have with a mapmaker from long ago to explain how GPS works. Use information from both passages to make your description clear.

_____

_____

_____

_____

_____

44

On the Move

Have you ever moved to another place? Every day, someone moves from one home to another. People change cities. They may move from the city to the country and back again. Some people move to different states. Others move to new countries. For as long as people have been on the planet, people have moved around.

Human **migration** happens when people move from one place to another. Sometimes, a group of people may decide to move together. In the 1600s, some people began leaving England. Many settled in the American colonies. Some moved for religious freedom. Others moved for better opportunities. Still others moved to have adventures. These are some of the same reasons that people move around today.

People migrate for many other reasons. War can cause some people to move. Families may move away from a place that is no longer safe. Sometimes, it is nature that causes people to leave their homes. Droughts, or long periods of time with no rain, mean that crops cannot grow. This can lead to **famine**. People have to move to find enough food. Hurricanes and floods can also force people from their homes. People may return and rebuild in the same places. But many times, they do not.

As long as people are on Earth, movement will happen. People will always want to live in places where they can have better lives.

Animals That Migrate

It is an early autumn day, and the temperature is getting cooler. High in the sky, a flock of geese are flying south. The birds are migrating, or moving from one place to another. Why do birds do this? Where are they going?

Birds migrate to survive. They go where the winter is warmer. They fly to places with more food. In the spring, when birds return home, nuts, seeds, and berries are **abundant** again.

A key reason that animals migrate is to find food. African elephants make long journeys to find food and water. Herds of Arctic caribou wander south to forests each winter. When spring arrives, they head north again.

Migrating fruit bats in Africa provide a stunning sight. More than eight million bats migrate seasonally to fill up on ripe fruit. The bats thicken the air as they swoop in to eat sweet bananas, mangoes, and other fruit. A fruit bat will eat double its body weight each night.

The animal that migrates the farthest is the humpback whale. Each year, humpback whales leave cold ocean waters and travel to warmer climates. When warm temperatures return, the whales swim back. The round-trip journey can cover over 10,000 miles (16,093 km)!

In the air, on land, and by sea, animals move around. Migrating animals survive by moving to find food. They follow their instincts to survive.

Name _____

Answer the questions.

1. Which sentence best explains the word **migration**?

    A. Migration is moving from one place to another.
    B. Migration is something that animals do.
    C. Migration is another word for survival.
    D. When people migrate, they want better lives.

2. Write **true** or **false**.

    _____ According to "On the Move," people first began to migrate in the 1600s.

    _____ According to "Animals That Migrate," birds fly to warmer regions because they will find more food there.

3. In "Animals That Migrate," why do you think the author included the information about the humpback whale?

    _____

    _____

4. In "On the Move," why do you think the author included the information about hurricanes and floods?

    _____

    _____

5. What does the word **famine** mean as used in "On the Move"?

    _____

    _____

6. What does the word **abundant** mean as used in "Animals That Migrate"?

    _____

    _____

Name _____

7. Complete each chart with the main idea and key details from the passage.

On the Move

Main Idea		
Key Detail	Key Detail	Key Detail

Animals That Migrate

Main Idea		
Key Detail	Key Detail	Key Detail

8. Write a summary that compares human and animal migration. Use the information in the charts to tell ways that they are alike and different.

_____

_____

_____

_____

_____

Wearing Many Hats

Leonardo da Vinci was a man who wore many hats during his lifetime. He was an accomplished artist, scientist, and inventor. Da Vinci lived during a time called the Renaissance. This time in history, from about the early 1300s to the late 1500s, was an era of new ideas.

Da Vinci was born in Italy in 1452. Early on, he found that he loved to draw. He also had a deep interest in nature. As a young man, he sketched plants and animals. His landscapes looked as real as photographs. Human faces fascinated him too. He studied the way faces showed emotions. His famous painting, *Mona Lisa*, is a masterpiece. The subject's slight smile conveys complex feelings.

Da Vinci became interested in science. He wanted to know how things, such as the human body, worked. He sketched bones and muscles. He drew veins and heart valves. Da Vinci's notebooks reveal his many questions. They also reveal his odd handwriting. He wrote from the right to the left. He also wrote his letters backward. His words formed a reverse image that had to be read by holding it up to a mirror.

An interest in flight led da Vinci to sketch ideas for flying machines. One sketch included flapping wings. He watched birds in flight. He felt that humans should be able to fly too. Other sketches show ideas for a parachute, scuba gear, and a robot. In so many ways, Leonardo da Vinci was a man ahead of his time.

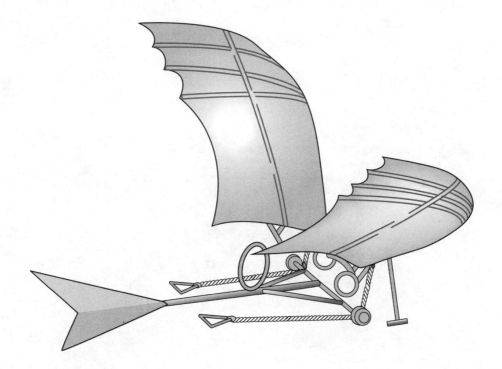

The Wright Brothers

Two young brothers played together at their home in Dayton, Ohio. The year was 1878. The boys' father had given them a flying toy powered by rubber bands. Orville and Wilbur Wright were interested in anything that could fly. Even a flock of birds caught their attention. Their deep interest in flying would one day change the world.

As young boys, Orville and Wilbur began making and selling kites. They trimmed the kites' wooden ribs to make them thinner. The kites were lighter too. The boys' friends began buying their kites because the kites flew so well.

In 1889, Orville and Wilbur became interested in publishing a newspaper. But, publishing did not provide enough income, and they had to give it up. Their next venture together was a bicycle shop. They started by repairing bicycles. Then, they began to see ways to improve them. Soon, they were building and selling their own bicycles.

The Wright Brothers had never lost their interest in flight. They read about people who were building and flying gliders. The brothers improved the design. They figured out a way to add controls. But, the gliders needed wind to fly.

Orville and Wilbur wanted to find a better way to power their flying machine. The answer was an engine that ran on gasoline. In December 1903, the Wright Brothers flew the first powered flying machine in Kitty Hawk, North Carolina. The brothers, who once envied the birds in the sky, flew! Their flight changed the way people would travel the world.

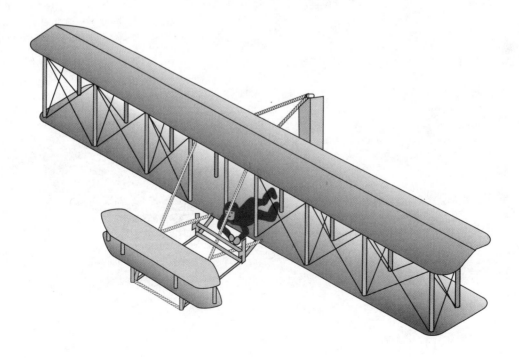

Name _____

Answer the questions.

1. What was the author's purpose in writing "Wearing Many Hats"?

   A. to explain what the Renaissance was like

   B. to describe how da Vinci learned to paint

   C. to persuade readers that da Vinci was the world's greatest artist

   D. to give information about Leonardo da Vinci's life

2. What was the author's purpose in writing "The Wright Brothers"?

   A. to compare the different ways the brothers worked

   B. to give information about the lives of Orville and Wilbur Wright

   C. to show how early failures can lead to later success

   D. to describe the Wright Brothers' first powered flight

3. Why did the Wright Brothers begin building bicycles?

   A. They wanted to make more money.

   B. They did not like the bicycles that broke down.

   C. They felt they could make better bicycles.

   D. They did not have equipment to repair bicycles.

Use the words in the word bank to complete the sentences.

> Leonardo da Vinci   Orville and Wilbur Wright

4. _____ made sketches of things in nature.

5. _____ published newspapers.

6. _____ had an interest in flying from an early age.

7. _____ became interested in both art and inventions.

Name _____

8. Complete the chart to compare Leonardo da Vinci with Orville and Wilbur Wright.

	Leonardo da Vinci	**Orville and Wilbur Wright**
Early Life		
Major Accomplishments		
Interesting Facts		

9. Imagine that Leonardo da Vinci and the Wright Brothers had lived at the same time. How do you think they would have felt about each other? Use facts and information from both passages to support your answer.

_____

_____

_____

_____

_____

_____

52

Keeping Balance

An ecosystem is a kind of community. It is made up of living things such as plants and animals. Nonliving things such as weather, soil, and climate are also important parts of an ecosystem. The living and nonliving parts depend on each other to survive.

An ecosystem can be small. Think of a pond. Fish swim in the water. Turtles burrow into the mud. Frogs leap out of the water onto lily pads. Cattails grow at the edge of the pond. Insects buzz in and around the plants. The sunshine is also a part of a pond's ecosystem. The soil the plants grow in is too. When the ecosystem is in balance, the pond is healthy. But, what if a drought occurs? Without enough rainfall, the pond could become dry. Some species would die.

Tropical rain forests are large ecosystems. About half of Earth's plant and animal species live in rain forests. Rain forest trees create about 40 percent of Earth's oxygen. About one-fifth of our freshwater supply can be found there. But, rain forest health is being threatened. People are clearing land for farms. Pollution harms plant and animal life. Experts are seeking ways to repair the harm that has been done.

Balance in an ecosystem is vital. Natural events, such as floods and droughts, can upset this balance. People, however, pose a bigger threat. As ecosystems decline, plants and animals disappear. Our world is forever changed when this happens.

Bringing Back the Wolves

During the 1800s, many people in the United States began to move west. At night, these early settlers could hear the howls of wolves in the distance. But, this changed over the next 100 years. The wolves' howls were heard less and less. What silenced the wolves as people began pushing westward?

When people settled in the west, they cleared land to build houses and grow crops. As settlers moved in, they pushed the wolves out of their natural **habitats**. Wolves are predators. They feed on animals as large as elk and deer and as small as rabbits and beavers. Now, hungry wolves began to attack the settlers' cattle, sheep, and chickens. And, of course, the settlers fought back.

When the number of wolves decreased, the ecosystem became out of balance. The number of elk and deer exploded. The number of rabbits and beavers increased too. These are animals that eat plants. Without wolves to keep their numbers in check, the animals began to run out of food. Entire groves of trees and shrubs disappeared from the landscape.

Over time, park rangers in Yellowstone National Park noticed these changes. Experts studied the ecosystem. They concluded that the problems started when wolves began to disappear.

In 1975, experts put a program in place to bring wolves back to the area. Today, the balance has been restored. The numbers of predators and prey are in check. Once again, wolves can be heard howling at night.

Name _____

Answer the questions.

1. What was the author's purpose in writing "Keeping Balance"?

    A. to give information about what pond life is like

    B. to persuade readers that pollution is harmful

    C. to describe ways that people can help save the rain forests

    D. to explain that ecosystems must be balanced to be healthy

2. What was the author's purpose in writing "Bringing Back the Wolves"?

    A. to compare wolves to the farm animals brought by the settlers

    B. to explain what happened when wolves began to disappear

    C. to show how early settlers lived

    D. to describe ways that wolves survive in the wild

3. Which statement best states a central idea in both passages?

    A. Balance in an ecosystem is very important.

    B. Ecosystems are complicated.

    C. People pose the only threat to ecosystems.

    D. It is too late to save many ecosystems.

4. Write **true** or **false**.

_____ According to "Keeping Balance," an ecosystem is a large community made up of plants and animals.

_____ According to "Bringing Back the Wolves," clearing land to build houses and grow crops contributed to the decline of wolves.

5. According to "Keeping Balance," what are the two major threats to ecosystems?

_____

6. What does the word **habitat** mean as it is used in "Bringing Back the Wolves"?

_____

Name _____

7. Complete the graphic organizer with facts and information about ecosystems that you learned from both passages.

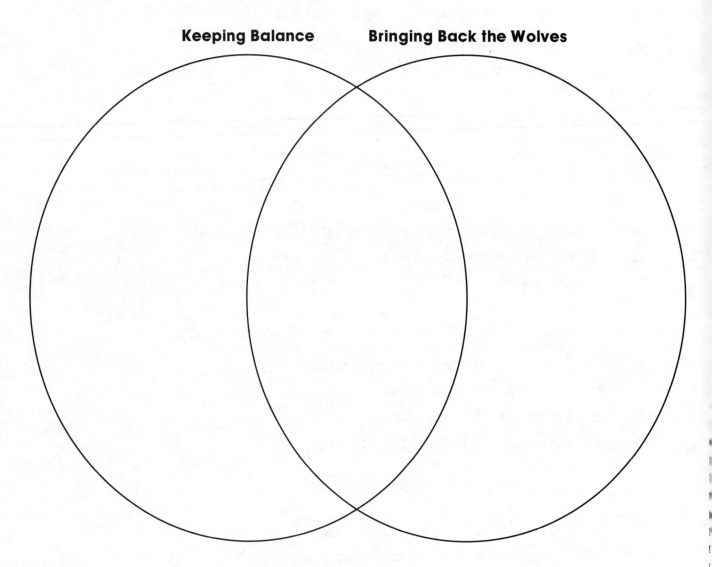

Keeping Balance   **Bringing Back the Wolves**

8. Which passage do you think gave more information about what an ecosystem is like? Use details from the text to support your opinion.

_____

_____

_____

_____

_____

_____

56

Cool Animal Tools

Have you ever seen an animal use a tool? If you are thinking about hammers and saws, then your answer is probably no. But, a tool can be anything that people and animals use to solve a problem. Let's look at some ways that really clever animals use tools!

Animal experts wanted to know just how smart crows are. They gave a crow a narrow jug of water. But, the water level was too low for the crow to reach with its beak. The animal experts had placed some pebbles nearby. The crow picked up and dropped pebbles into the jug to raise the water level so that it could drink. A crow is a smart bird!

If you have ever been stung by a wasp, you know how painful that can be! Wasps sting to protect themselves. But, they have other ways of staying safe too. A digger wasp builds a nest underground. To hide the entrance from predators, it flies over the opening and drops in gravel, dried leaves, and sticks.

Capuchin monkeys like to eat palm nuts, but how do they crack them open? These smart guys smash the nuts with stones. They have even been observed trying several different stones to find one that is the right weight for the job!

For a long time, scientists believed that only people were intelligent enough to use tools to solve problems. Today, they are beginning to see that some pretty smart animals are out there doing amazing things with tools!

Picking Up a Stone

About three million years ago, early humans figured out how to use tools, items to help them solve problems. This period of time was called the Stone Age. The name referred to the fact that many early tools were made from stones. The Stone Age was made up of three periods: early, middle, and late.

The Early Stone Age era began when a human first picked up a stone and used it. Its use was most likely to kill an animal for food. At some point, early humans determined how to shape stones by hitting them with harder stones. The oldest stone tools ever found are called hammerstones. The name refers to how the stones were used.

The Middle Stone Age was a time when tools became smaller. People sharpened some stones into points. They added points to handles or shafts of wood to make spears. They sharpened the edges of stones to make scrapers. These were helpful in cleaning animal skins.

During the Late Stone Age, people became skillful at making tools from other materials. For example, people used bone needles to stitch skins together to make clothing. They also used ivory and wood. However, these materials were not as permanent as stone.

The Stone Age lasted about 2.5 million years. Early humans used stone tools to help them meet their **basic needs**. Then, people began making tools from metal, ushering in the Bronze Age.

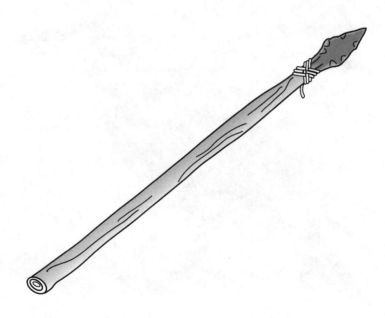

Name _____

Answer the questions.

1. What would be another good title for "Cool Animal Tools"?

   A. Which Animal Is the Smartest?

   B. How Crows Drink Water

   C. Animals Solving Problems

   D. Animal Experts at Work

2. What would be another good title for "Picking Up a Stone"?

   A. Stone Age Tools   **B.** The Early Stone Age

   C. Making Spears   **D.** Why the Stone Age Ended

3. According to "Cool Animal Tools," a crow used pebbles to

   A. hide the place where he gets water.

   B. break the jug so that he could get water.

   C. cause the water in the jug to rise.

   D. stand on so that he could reach the water.

4. According to "Picking Up a Stone," the Middle Stone Age was a time when

   A. metal tools were first made.

   B. the first person used a tool to solve a problem.

   C. people made tools from bone, ivory, and wood.

   D. early humans made sharp points for spears.

5. What do the words **basic needs** mean as they are used in the last paragraph of "Picking Up a Stone"?

   _____

   _____

6. In "Picking Up a Stone," how did the author define tools?

   _____

   _____

7. Key details are important pieces of information that can lead you to the main idea. Complete the chart with three key details from each passage. Use the details to help you determine the main idea of each passage.

Cool Animal Tools			Picking Up a Stone		
Key Detail	Key Detail	Key Detail	Key Detail	Key Detail	Key Detail
Main Idea			Main Idea		

8. Use the information in the chart to write a summary about a central idea that is common to both passages.

_____

_____

_____

_____

_____

_____

The Top of the World

The Arctic Circle is the northernmost region of planet Earth. Imagine your head as the planet. If you place your palm on top of your head, you are covering the Arctic Circle. This chilly area is made up of the Arctic Ocean surrounded by frozen land. The average winter temperature is -40°F (-40°C). So, who lives in this icy land that sees little sunlight for half the year?

The Inuits are one group of people who call this frosty land their home. Many Inuits live in Greenland. This large island lies almost completely within the Arctic Circle. More than three-fourths of Greenland is covered by a thick sheet of ice. Living in such a harsh climate is not easy. Yet, for thousands of years, people have found ways to adapt and survive.

Arctic animals have found many ways to adapt to this challenging land as well. The arctic fox has a white coat in the winter that blends in with the snow. The fox's coat keeps it safe from polar bears. A walrus has a long ivory tusk. This tusk is a weapon against predators. Snowy owls have plumage, or feathers, that change with the seasons. Blending in with the landscape allows the owls to sneak up on their prey.

The white and frozen Arctic is like an icy crown at the top of the world. This vast, **forbidding** land is a challenge to all who call it home. Yet, both humans and animals survive and even thrive there.

Unicorns of the Sea

A unicorn is a mythical creature. This means it has never existed. But the narwhal, often called the unicorn of the sea, does exist. Imagine a whale with a unicorn-like horn on its face. Of the world's whales, the narwhal is the rarest.

Like other whales, a narwhal is a mammal. Mammals have hair on their bodies and produce milk to feed their young. These seldom-seen creatures live in the icy waters of the Arctic. Swimming mostly at the surface of the ocean, narwhals can dive quite deeply when they need to.

The narwhal's most unusual feature is a horn. But, it is not actually a horn. It is really a long spiral tooth. Mostly male narwhals grow this long tooth, which can reach lengths of 9 feet (2.7 m). The teeth of most animals have a hard exterior and a soft core. The narwhal's tooth is just the opposite. It has soft outside tissue and a hard inner core. This makes the long tooth flexible. The narwhal's tooth can bend without breaking.

Narwhals travel in groups. Like many other whales, they communicate by making clicking or squealing sounds to each other. Narwhals feed on shrimp, squid, and fish. Both orcas and polar bears hunt narwhals for food.

Unlike the unicorn of legend, the mysterious narwhal is a real creature. Threats to the narwhal's habitat from pollution and climate change are also real. Experts are studying ways to protect narwhals so that they are with us for a long time.

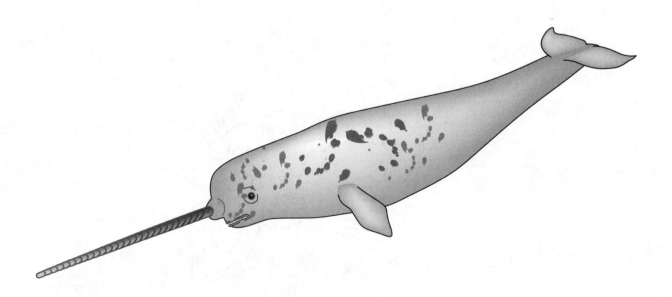

Name _____

Answer the questions.

1. What was the author's purpose in writing "The Top of the World"?

   A. to persuade readers to visit the Arctic

   B. to give information about life in the Arctic

   C. to explain how some animals have adapted to the Arctic

   D. to describe what winter is like in the Arctic

2. What was the author's purpose in writing "Unicorns of the Sea"?

   A. to tell what narwhals are like and where they live

   B. to describe a narwhal's long tooth

   C. to compare unicorns and narwhals

   D. to give information about threats to narwhals

3. According to "The Top of the World," what do people and animals in the Arctic have in common?

   A. Both have ways of blending in with the landscape.

   B. Both migrate to warmer regions in the winter.

   C. Both have adapted to the Arctic climate.

   D. Both live in Greenland.

4. Write **true** or **false**.

   _____ The Arctic region is made up of frozen land surrounded by water.

   _____ Narwhals are able to communicate with each other.

5. What is an important difference between a narwhal's tooth and the teeth of most other animals?

   _____

   _____

6. What does the word **forbidding** mean as it is used in "The Top of the World"?

   _____

Name _____

Choose the correct answer.

7. Think about the details in "The Top of the World" and "Unicorns of the Sea." Complete the chart to tell how these details lead you to a deeper understanding of the Arctic.

	The Top of the World	**Unicorns of the Sea**
I. What did I learn about the climate?		
2. What did I learn about Arctic life?		
3. What did I learn about threats to the Arctic?		

8. What else would you like to know about the Arctic? What are some questions that you feel were not answered by either passage?

_____

_____

_____

_____

_____

I Am the Wind

I lift the laundry on the line,

I dry it faster than sunshine.

I move sea waves in wisps of foam

and rattle the windows of your home.

You may look at the fluttering leaves on the tree,

but try as you might, you will never see me.

I often accompany the storm late at night,

I shriek, I howl, I cause terrible fright.

Morning comes and I am as silent as a ghost,

yet I've left a sign creaking on the old signpost.

I can flutter white sails and move boats 'cross the sea

and blow high your kite until it catches a tree.

I can blow strong and cold, I don't care to be weak,

I can lift off your hat and paint red on your cheek.

Where will I blow next? There is no way to tell.

A kite might fly high, or I might ring a bell.

We may never be friends in this world, you and I,

But, I will whisper warm greetings the next time I pass by.

Nana Ortiz and the Goblins

"We're going to see *goblins*?" I asked my grandmother. Nana Ortiz was probably the greatest grandmother in the world, but sometimes she thought of some pretty strange summer vacation ideas.

"You only heard part of it. We're going to Goblin Valley State Park," she explained. "It's in Utah and only a few hours away. So saddle up, Cowboy!"

Like I said, Nana Ortiz is a little unusual. My name is Henry, but when I visit her in Arizona, she insists on calling me Cowboy. The three-hour drive to the park was uneventful. And believe me, this is not usually the case when Nana Ortiz and I take a road trip. If she sees a sign for the world's biggest ball of string, you can bet that she will stop.

"What you're going to see," Nana explained. "is spectacular. These land features have been called mushrooms, hoodoos, and goblins. You'll see why soon enough."

I have to admit, I was excited when we finally arrived and I saw the strange rocks for the first time. I felt like I was on Mars! Nana said that a space movie was filmed there. She also told me how the rocks formed. More than 25 million years ago, water began to erode the softer rock. This left the harder rock behind. The wind shaped, smoothed, and rounded the stones over time.

Nana Ortiz and I have taken some amazing trips together. But, the day she took me to see the goblins was the best!

Answer the questions.

1. Is "I Am the Wind" fiction or nonfiction? Explain your answer.

_____

_____

2. What genre is "I Am the Wind"? How do you know?

_____

_____

3. Is "Nana Ortiz and the Goblins" fiction or nonfiction? Explain your answer.

_____

_____

4. What genre is "Nana Ortiz and the Goblins"? How do you know?

_____

_____

5. What did Nana mean when she said, "So saddle up, Cowboy!" in "Nana Ortiz and the Goblins"?

_____

_____

6. Why do you think the wind said, "We may never be friends in this world, you and I" in "I Am the Wind"?

_____

_____

7. In "Nana Ortiz and the Goblins," why do you think the author included the detail about Nana stopping for the world's biggest ball of string?

_____

_____

Name _____

8. Complete the chart to learn more about the characters in each passage.

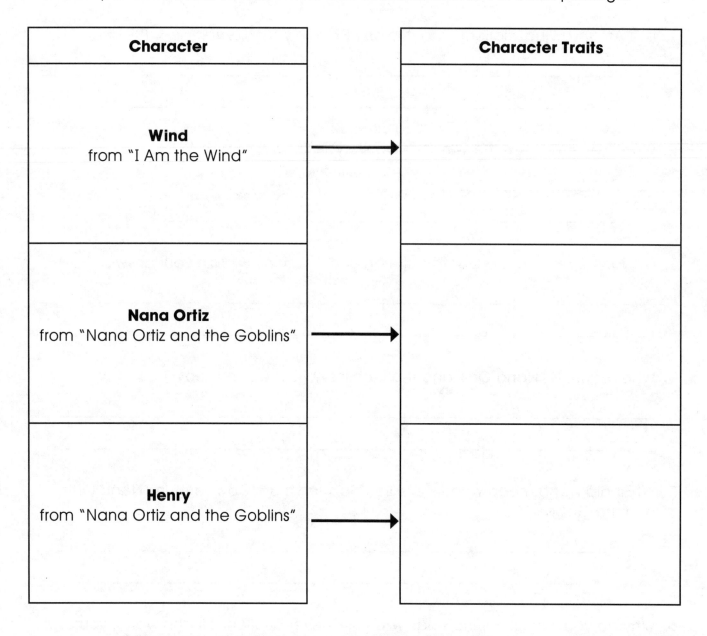

Character		Character Traits
Wind from "I Am the Wind"	→	
Nana Ortiz from "Nana Ortiz and the Goblins"	→	
Henry from "Nana Ortiz and the Goblins"	→	

9. What part did the wind play in the poem and in the realistic fiction piece? Write a paragraph that compares details about the wind from each passage.

_____

_____

_____

_____

_____

The Greedy King

Once, in a land long ago, lived a king who was known for his greedy nature. The people in his kingdom were farmers. But, they were quite poor because the king demanded half of their crops. The royal cook, Pilar, felt great sorrow as she prepared rich feasts for the king.

One evening, Pilar walked home to her small cottage, thinking about the king's greed. She was drawing water from her well, when a curious thing happened. She peered into the bucket expecting to find water. Instead, it contained 10 gold coins! Surprised but grateful, Pilar knew exactly what she would do with her newfound wealth.

The next day, she distributed nine coins to nine hungry villagers. Day after day, Pilar retrieved gold coins from the well and day after day, she gave away nine coins.

One day, the king heard this news. He followed Pilar to learn where this wealth came from. How surprised he was to find out!

"This is my kingdom! These coins are mine!" he bellowed. He grabbed the bucket from Pilar and dropped it into the well. But, when he pulled it up, it contained only water. He tried seven times, but he retrieved only water each time.

"The coins must be down there!" he cried. Before Pilar could stop him, the king jumped into the well. The well was so deep that Pilar did not even hear a splash. The greedy king was never heard from again.

Buried Treasure

"Is this a weed?" I asked, pointing to a fuzzy green plant with spikes. I didn't mind helping Mom weed the garden, especially because she was paying me and I needed the money. I **had my eye on** a 20-dollar video game at Video Exchange, but at 10 cents a weed, it would take me a million years to earn enough. But, it was summer vacation, and I had nothing better happening.

"That's definitely a weed, Rudy," she said. I pushed the spade into the ground, lifted the weed from the soil, and dropped it into the basket. When I did, a sparkly ring winked at me from the tangled, dirty roots.

"Mom!" I called. "Look at this!" Mom examined it closely and found an inscription inside the band. "To Maggie with Love," she read. "This must be Mrs. Rinaldi's. Her first name is Maggie."

Mom and Dad had bought our house the year before from Mr. and Mrs. Rinaldi, who now lived in a smaller house across the park. "Let's take it over!" I said.

Mrs. Rinaldi was surprised to see us. But, when I showed her the ring and explained where we found it, she began to cry. It had been a special anniversary gift. After she lost it, she never expected to see it again.

"Please accept this small reward," she said, handing me a 20-dollar bill. But, I wouldn't take it. "I'm making enough money," I told her, "and, who knows, maybe I'll dig up more treasure!"

Name _____

Answer the questions.

1. What was the author's purpose in writing "The Greedy King"?

   A. to show how kings lived long ago

   B. to describe the problems the villagers had

   C. to teach a lesson about being greedy

   D. to explain how water wells worked

2. According to "The Greedy King," why did Pilar feel great sorrow when she prepared the king's feasts?

   A. Preparing the feasts was hard work.

   B. She was not allowed to eat when she was cooking.

   C. The king made her work long hours.

   D. She knew that the villagers were hungry.

3. What does the phrase **had my eye on** mean as it is used in the first paragraph of "Buried Treasure"?

   A. had seen it and wanted it   **B.** had not seen it yet

   C. planned to go see it   **D.** will see it one day

4. What would be another good title for "Buried Treasure"?

   A. Across the Park   **B.** Video Exchange

   C. Doing the Right Thing   **D.** Rudy Helps Mom

5. What would be another good title for "The Greedy King"?

   A. Pilar's Small Cottage   **B.** The Hungry Villagers

   C. The King's Feast   **D.** The Generous Cook

6. Write **true** or **false**.

   _____ Pilar gave away nine coins and kept one.

7. Write **true** or **false**.

   _____ Rudy used Mrs. Rinaldi's money to buy a video game.

Name _____

8. Think about the characters in both passages. What were their actions? What motivated the characters to take the actions they did? Complete the chart to learn more about the characters and their motivations.

Who?	Did What?	Why?
the King from "The Greedy King"	jumped into the well	
Pilar from "The Greedy King"		She wanted to help the villagers.
Mom from "Buried Treasure"		She needed help in the garden.
Rudy from "Buried Treasure"	returned the ring to Mrs. Rinaldi	

9. Use the information in the chart to compare the king from "The Greedy King" to Rudy in "Buried Treasure." Which character is your favorite? Write a paragraph that explains why.

_____

_____

_____

_____

Baboon and Ant

There once was a baboon that lived in a land of ripe bananas and sweet mangoes. Baboon liked pounding his chest and acting very important. Most of the animals did not mind this because Baboon could be helpful when he wanted to be.

For example, Giraffe once hurt her neck and could not reach the high leaves on the palm tree. Baboon shimmied up the tall tree and snatched leaves for Giraffe's next three meals. Another time, a tiger cub became stranded in the river where rising floodwaters threatened to sweep the cub away. Baboon swung over the water and rescued the cub. Yes, Baboon was often kind, but sometimes he was not.

Each day, Ant worked hard to build an anthill. She pushed sand into place until her home was just right. But, if Baboon spotted the anthill, he would kick it over. Poor Ant would have to begin again.

Ant reasoned with Baboon, but he would not listen. He said that Ant was so small that kicking her anthill was of no consequence.

One day when Baboon napped, Ant crawled inside his ear. She marched around while Baboon wriggled and jumped. What enormous thing was in his ear? He shook his head trying to dislodge whatever was there.

Finally, Ant spoke. "Do I have your attention?" Baboon indicated that he did.

"If you ever wish to nap peacefully again," Ant shouted, "you will stop kicking my anthill!"

From that day forward, Baboon carefully stepped around any anthill he saw.

The Tower of Blocks

"I'll only be gone an hour," Mom said. "Remember, Mason, you're his older brother, and he's only five. So, please have a little more patience with him, OK?"

"Sure, Mom," I said. "Don't worry. We'll be fine."

As Mom left with the casserole for Aunt Delia, I grabbed my book and plopped down on the sofa.

Nicholas was on the floor with about a thousand blocks. Building towers was his favorite activity. He was actually good at stacking blocks pretty high before they fell over.

"Hey, Mason," he said, looking up, "make a tower with me, OK?"

I looked over and saw that he had built a wide base and was now stacking the blocks in a kind of elaborate zigzag pattern that was already pretty tall.

"Not right now, I'm reading," I explained.

"Come on and play with me," he begged. "Let's build a tower that touches the ceiling!"

"I'm reading!" I said again. "Mom didn't say I had to play with you but just watch you." I shifted around on the sofa and when I did, I dropped my book right onto Nicholas's tower. *Crash*! The blocks tumbled to the ground.

"Hey, I'm sorry," I said. "That was an accident." Nicholas did not say anything but just started gathering the blocks that had skittered across the floor. His head was down, and I thought I saw him wipe a tear.

"I'll get the ones that went under the sofa," I told him. "Then, we'll build a tower that touches the ceiling!"

Name _____

Answer the questions.

1. Describe the setting of "Baboon and Ant."

   _____

   _____

2. Describe the setting of "The Tower of Blocks."

   _____

   _____

3. What did the author mean by writing, "Baboon liked pounding his chest and acting very important" in the first paragraph of "Baboon and Ant"?

   _____

   _____

4. In "The Tower of Blocks," why do you think Mom asked Mason to have more patience with Nicholas?

   _____

   _____

5. In "Baboon and Ant," Ant finally got Baboon to listen by

   A. asking Giraffe to speak to him.

   B. crawling inside his ear.

   C. reasoning with Baboon.

   D. telling Baboon to be kinder.

6. In "The Tower of Blocks," Nicholas picked up his blocks without speaking to Mason because

   A. he did not understand what happened to the tower.

   B. he felt that Mason did not want him to speak.

   C. he knew that Mason knocked the tower over on purpose.

   D. he was upset that Mason knocked over the tower.

Name _____

7. Words and actions help readers learn more about what story characters are like. Think about the words and actions of Baboon and Mason in the two passages. Complete the chart to tell how both characters changed.

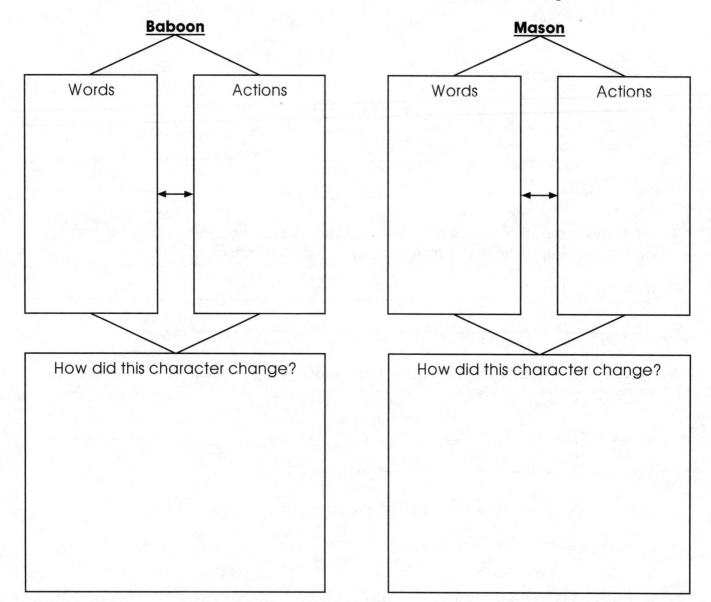

Baboon

Words | Actions

How did this character change?

Mason

Words | Actions

How did this character change?

8. What was the main reason that each character changed? Write a summary that tells the cause for each change.

_____

_____

_____

_____

_____

The New Girl

I looked around the cafeteria as small groups of kids laughed and headed toward the tables together. I was standing there holding my lunch bag, thinking about where I should sit, when someone tapped me on the shoulder.

"Do you want to have lunch with us?" a girl from class asked. "I'm Yasmin, by the way, and this is Lindsey."

"I'm Olivia," I said. "But, I guess you already know that because Mr. Tanaka wrote it in big letters on the board this morning."

Yasmin laughed and then nodded toward a table. We sat at the table and began to eat. "Where did you move from?" she asked me.

"Phoenix, Arizona," I said. "My dad got transferred. This is the first time I've ever changed schools."

"This is my third school," Lindsey said, "And, I hope it's my last."

"I've never moved," Yasmin said. "I always thought it would be exciting to live somewhere else."

"It is exciting," I agreed. "But, it is scary and actually sad too. In fact, I think that moving to a new place probably brings up just about any emotions anyone could ever have."

Lindsey nodded her head. "You forgot to mention anger. I was pretty upset when my mom first told me we were moving again. I kept asking her if getting a promotion was actually worth it."

Yasmin smiled. "This may sound a little selfish," she said, "but I'm happy that you're both here, because I think we're going to be great friends. Just don't ever move again!"

From Planet Zeron

As the silvery spaceship touched down lightly on a grassy area, three emerald green faces peered out the window. "It looks enjoyable here," Rix reported. "I think we will like living on this planet."

"Absolutely," Mother ChipChop replied. "Planet Zeron was overcrowded. Planet Earth looks like it has much more room."

"And much to do," Father ChipChop said. "Rix, the building you see is a school, a place where Earthlings learn things. You can go in there now while we find a home. Then, we will come back for you at the end of the school day." Father ChipChop opened the hatch, and Rix walked down the steps. Immediately, the shiny spaceship took off.

Suddenly a bell rang, startling Rix. The school doors opened, and boys and girls poured out. Some held small bags, while others carried rectangular boxes covered in colorful pictures. They began filling up the tables in a courtyard.

A boy noticed Rix standing nearby. "Are you new?" he asked. "I'm Caleb. Do you want to sit with us?"

Rix followed Caleb to a table. "You don't have any lunch today?" Caleb asked. "Lucky for you! My mom always makes a gigantic lunch. Here's a sandwich and some juice."

"Thank you," Rix said. "Are all Earth people as generous as you?"

"I don't know," Caleb laughed, "because I don't know all of the people on Earth!" Rix laughed too.

As he sipped the delicious juice and bit into the tuna sandwich, Rix thought how very **fortunate** he was that his parents had moved to Earth.

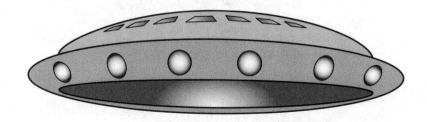

Name _____

Answer the questions.

1. Is "The New Girl" realistic fiction or science fiction? How do you know?

   _____

   _____

2. Is "From Planet Zeron" realistic fiction or science fiction? How do you know?

   _____

   _____

3. What do Yasmin from "The New Girl" and Caleb from "From Planet Zeron" have in common?

   A. Both like to hear interesting stories.   **B.** Both have moved around a lot.

   C. Both are kind to new people.   **D.** Both know what to bring for lunch.

4. What can you learn about Lindsey from "The New Girl" when she said, "And, I hope it's my last"?

   A. She feels that moving is exciting.

   B. She's glad that Olivia moved there.

   C. She does not like the school.

   D. She does not want to move again.

5. In "The New Girl," what is a likely reason that Olivia said that a move can be sad?

   A. It can be sad to move away from friends.

   B. Olivia does not want to leave her new school.

   C. It can be sad when no one listens to you.

   D. Olivia begged her dad not to leave Arizona.

6. What does the word **fortunate** mean as it is used in the last paragraph of "From Planet Zeron."

   A. confused   **B.** lucky

   C. tricky   **D.** generous

Name _____

7. Thinking about when events happen helps readers better understand a story. Complete the graphic organizer with important details that happened in the beginning, middle, and end of each passage.

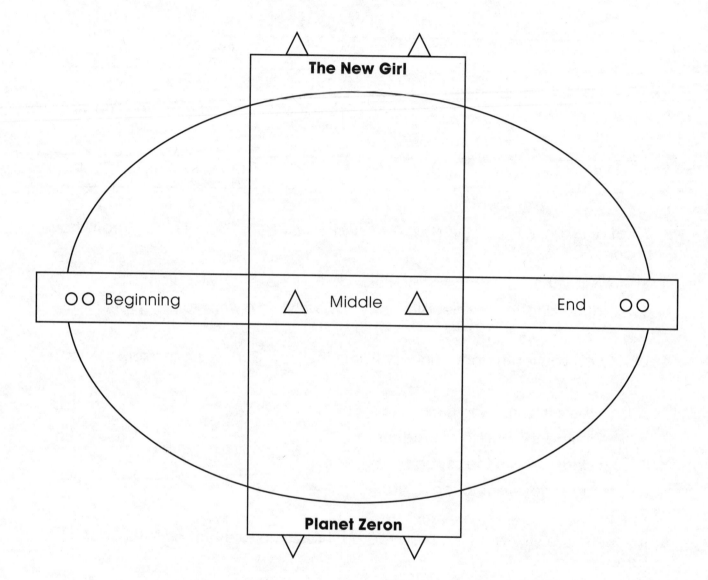

8. Is the central message of each passage the same or different? Write a summary that compares the central message in both passages.

_____

_____

_____

_____

_____

Fireflies

As sun goes down, lights blink on,

yellow twinkling night beams.

Summer evening, bits of gold,

fireflies flashing light dreams.

As night sky flickers brightly,

the little insects' call,

Hello! And how do you do?

Bright greetings for one and all!

The shimmering show begins now,

a dazzling, dizzy dance.

Fluorescent flings crisscross the sky

as an obliging cricket chants.

Pink dawn of morning, rising sun,

when fireflies flit away,

until dark night descends once more

to signal their starry ballet.

The Light Show

Elijah did not want to spend the summer in Tennessee. He had begged his parents to let him stay with his friend in Brooklyn. But, it was no surprise that they said no.

"Julio's grandmother is having a birthday party! His family is doing a big fireworks show!" I told them. Still, his parents said no.

It is not that Uncle Graham was not fun to be around, because he was. And, he lived in a cool log cabin in the mountains. Still, Elijah hated missing fireworks in Brooklyn.

"I've got several hikes planned," his uncle said when he arrived, "and one pretty spectacular light show!"

"Fireworks?" Elijah asked. Maybe his parents had told Uncle Graham that he was missing a fireworks show to be in Tennessee.

"Not fireworks, exactly," Uncle Graham said. "You'll see. It's tomorrow night."

The next evening, Uncle Graham and Elijah headed out. Dozens of people joined them on the trail as they walked deeper into the forest. Finally, in a clearing, they sat down.

"Strange place for fireworks," Elijah said. At that moment, he saw his first firefly. Its silvery light pierced the darkness among the trees. Then, another and another lit up the night. There must have been thousands. But, what astonished Elijah the most was the way they blinked in unison.

All around them, fireflies flashed together as if putting on a show just for them. Elijah noticed patterns such as three quick flashes and then darkness. For two hours, the fireflies flashed their greetings. And, Elijah did not miss Brooklyn at all.

Name _____

Answer the questions.

1. Is "Fireflies" fiction or nonfiction? Explain your answer.

_____

_____

2. What genre is "Fireflies"? How do you know?

_____

_____

3. Is "The Light Show" fiction or nonfiction? Explain your answer.

_____

_____

4. What genre is "The Light Show"? How do you know?

_____

_____

5. In "Fireflies," what does the author compare fireflies coming out at night to?

_____

_____

6. In "The Light Show," why did Uncle Graham say, "Not fireworks, exactly"?

_____

_____

7. Alliteration is when several words begin with the same sound or letters. Poems sometimes include alliteration. What are some examples of alliteration in "Fireflies"?

_____

_____

Name _____

8. Descriptive words help readers visualize, or picture, an event. Complete the graphic organizer with words or phrases that the authors used to help you picture the fireflies in both the poem and the fiction piece.

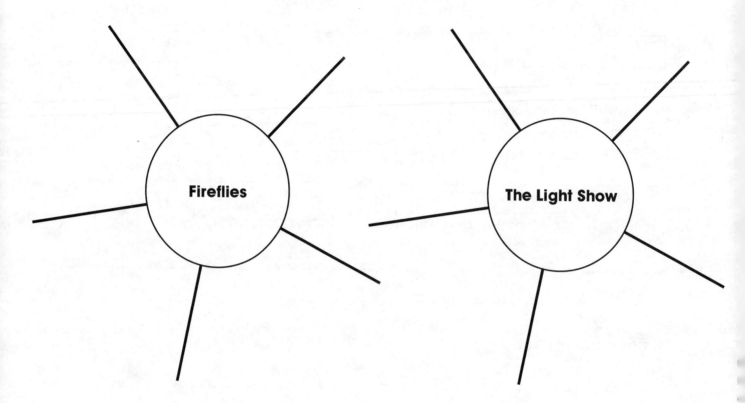

9. Do you think the poem or the fiction piece was more effective in helping you visualize fireflies? Write a paragraph to explain your answer.

_____
_____
_____
_____
_____
_____
_____
_____
_____
_____

Help, Please

Not everyone believes the story of Betsy Ross, the woman who made America's first flag. Some say it is just a tale, but I was there. I may only be a little mouse, but I know what I saw.

Mrs. Ross had a small sewing shop in Philadelphia, and when she was busy, she often ate lunch there. One day, I smelled fresh bread. Mrs. Ross was having my favorite lunch with some salty cheese. You may not know this, but Mrs. Ross was a little messy. This meant plenty of crumbs, which is why I was hanging around on the day in question.

The door flew open with such a clatter that I dropped my cheese. I peered up and saw the great man himself, General George Washington! Mrs. Ross asked what she could do for him.

General Washington explained that the new country had no flag, and this just would not do! He asked Mrs. Ross for her help. General Washington showed her a sketch. She frowned at the six-pointed stars the general had drawn and then made a few suggestions.

After he left, Mrs. Ross got to work. Bright scraps of red, white, and blue littered the floor as her scissors clicked and clacked into the night. Moonlight streamed in the window, reflecting off her silvery needle and fine thread. The flag grew larger with each stripe and star.

By morning, it was done. General Washington had tears in his eyes when he first saw it. And, I was there, a witness to history.

My Cooking Journal

Monday

It is my first day at cooking camp! I'm in the Yummy Sweets group. We started the day picking blueberries and eating a few too! They were warm from the sun. As I bit into them, I felt little berry explosions of sweet juice in my mouth. When we baked our muffins, the aroma of vanilla cake and blueberries floated over the whole camp!

Tuesday

A local farmer brought over fresh peaches. We peeled off the fuzzy skin and sliced them up for a pie. Making the piecrust was fun. We rolled out the silky dough into a big circle and placed it in the dish. Then, we poured in the peaches that were sprinkled with sugar. Finally, we put another crust on top and cut tiny slits into the top.

Wednesday

Today, we made watermelon ice pops! We scooped out the juicy red fruit and put it in a blender with some tart lime juice and sweet honey. Then, we poured the mixture into molds. The smell of watermelon always reminds me of a freshly mowed lawn. Maybe, it just makes me think of summer!

Thursday

My eyes are watering, my nose is running . . . and I'm enjoying every moment of it. I really like spicy food. It reminds me of the meals at my Tia Maria's table. We made quesadillas for dinner tonight. We each made our own, filling them with anything we wanted to include. The kitchen had all sorts of things to choose from, including cheese, bacon, sliced chicken, tomatoes, avocado, and two kinds of beans. Oh, and did I say there were jalapeños? That's why my nose is running!

Friday

I cannot believe this is my last day! We spent the first part of the day making thin sheets of gingerbread that we cut into squares. Then, we made homemade marshmallows that looked like fluffy white clouds! Next, we melted chocolate and poured it onto a marble slab. After it cooled, we broke it into pieces. Later, as the campfire crackled and popped, we made the world's best s'mores!

Name _____

Answer the questions.

1. Describe the setting of "Help, Please."

_____

_____

2. Describe the setting of "My Cooking Journal."

_____

_____

3. Who is the narrator in "Help, Please"? What can you learn about the narrator in the passage?

_____

_____

4. Who is the narrator in "My Cooking Journal"? What can you learn about the narrator in the passage?

_____

_____

5. In "Help, Please" Betsy Ross probably agreed to make the flag because

  A. she had grown tired of sewing clothing.

  B. she did not want to disappoint the general.

  C. she needed the money.

  D. she wanted to help her country.

6. Why do you think the narrator in "My Cooking Journal" wrote that watermelon made her think of summer?

  A. The smell reminded her of a freshly mowed lawn.

  B. She only eats watermelon in the summer.

  C. Watermelon is not available during winter months.

  D. Watermelon makes her remember summer camp.

7. Authors use details that appeal to our senses. Sensory details help us better visualize characters, settings, and events. Complete the chart with sensory details from both passages.

	Help, Please	**My Cooking Journal**
See		
Smell		
Hear		
Touch		
Taste		

8. Choose one sensory detail from each passage. Write a paragraph that tells whether you feel the details work. Explain why or why not. If not, how could the author have improved the details?

_____

_____

_____

_____

_____

Ice Cream!

It was 1904 and the St. Louis World's Fair **buzzed** with crowds of people enjoying the sights and sounds. My family had an ice cream booth. We had been selling bowls of ice cream almost as fast as we could make them.

I was in the back cranking the ice cream maker when I heard my Papa call out, "Emmett, count the paper cups!"

I looked at the stack in the corner and yelled, "Ten!" Quickly doing the math in my head, I knew this meant we had sold almost 500 cups of ice cream! Papa had known the treat would be popular, but it seems it was even more popular than he had imagined. Now, we were almost out of cups, and the day was only half over. I was thinking of the money we could be making when I caught a whiff of Mr. Yosef's sugary waffles baking in the next booth.

"I'll be right back!" I shouted and then ran next door to the waffle booth. I gave Mr. Yosef a dime, and he handed me a warm waffle wrapped in paper. I folded it into a cone shape. By the time I got it back to our booth, the waffle was cool. Papa watched in surprise as I dropped a large scoop of vanilla ice cream into the waffle cone.

"Genius!" Papa cried and kissed me on the head. Then, he hurried next door and bought stacks of Mr. Yosef's waffles.

The City Blizzard

Pablo looked through the window at the blowing snow and could not even see the building across the street. The stoop was covered to the top step. Not one carriage had passed by for over an hour because horses could not get through the streets. The blizzard had shut down New York City.

Pablo's mother called from her bedroom. He winced at her raspy cough. "Yes, Mother?" Pablo said. His heart quickened when he saw that she appeared even weaker than before.

"I need you to run to Dr. Upton's," she whispered hoarsely, holding an empty amber medicine bottle. Pablo glanced at the window's closed curtains. Mother did not know about the blizzard!

If she knew, she would not let him go. But, Mother needed the medicine. "I'm leaving now!" he cried. Pablo pulled on his heaviest winter clothing. Just before pushing the door open, he saw a ball of red yarn in Mother's knitting basket. He grabbed it and went out into the blinding snow.

With difficulty, Pablo tied the end of the yarn to the doorknob. As he made his way down the street, he tied the yarn from tree to tree as the howling wind stung his cheeks. Finally, he reached Dr. Upton's place.

With the medicine in his pocket, Pablo was on his way. Hand over hand on the red yarn, he found his way home, despite the fact that he could see no more than an inch or two in front of him.

Name _____

Answer the questions.

1. In "Ice Cream!," why did Papa ask Emmett to count the paper cups?

   A. Someone wanted to buy the extra paper cups.

   B. Emmett was supposed to count the cups every hour.

   C. They were almost out of cups, and Papa needed to know how many were left.

   D. Papa wanted to know if he needed to buy more cups.

2. In "The City Blizzard," why was Pablo unable to see the building across the street?

   A. The sun had gone down.   **B.** The building had been torn down.

   C. He could not find his eyeglasses.   **D.** The snow was falling hard and thick.

3. Why does the author use the word **buzzed** in the first paragraph of "Ice Cream"?

   A. to show how much people like ice cream

   B. to tell how the crowds of people sound

   C. to explain that bees are at the World's Fair

   D. to describe how quiet the crowds are

4. In "The City Blizzard," why didn't Pablo tell Mother about the blizzard?

   A. She would not let him go out to get the medicine.

   B. Seeing that much snow would upset his mother.

   C. She might ask him to shovel the walk.

   D. She would not let him go out to play with his friends.

5. Describe the event in "Ice Cream" that gave Emmett the idea to buy waffles.

   _____

   _____

6. Describe the event in "The City Blizzard" that helped Pablo safely find his way through the blizzard.

   _____

   _____

Name _____

7. Story characters often have to work through a problem or overcome a difficulty. This makes the story more interesting to readers. Complete the chart to better understand the problem and solution in each passage.

	Problem	Solution
Ice Cream!		
The City Blizzard		

8. Write a paragraph that describes the characters who solved the problems in each story.

_____

_____

_____

_____

_____

_____

Answer Key

Pages 7–8

1. C; 2. B; 3. B; 4. D; 5. Answers will vary but should include that the story teaches that boasting is a quality that is not appreciated by others. 6. Answers will vary but should include details that demonstrate an understanding that *metamorphosis* is the change that takes place when a tadpole becomes a frog.
7. Answers will vary but should include details from the passages such as: (How Old Frog changed) *At first*: Old Frog had a beautiful tail. *Then*: Old Frog boasted about his tail. *Finally*: Old Frog lost his tail. (How all frogs change) *At first*: A frog lays eggs in the water. *Then*: The eggs hatch, and tadpoles swim in the water. *Finally*: The tadpoles change into frogs that move onto the land.
8. Answers will vary but should include that both passages show changes that take place in the lives of frogs. 9. Answers will vary but should include details that explain that "Old Frog's Tail" is fiction that tells a story about how frogs change, while "Tadpole to Frog" is nonfiction and includes facts about how frogs change.

Pages 11–12

1. fiction; Answers will vary but should include that the story is fiction because it describes events that did not really happen. 2. Nonfiction; Answers will vary but should include that the text is nonfiction because it is based on facts and information about Iceland. 3. C; 4. D; 5. A; 6. false; Answers will vary but should include evidence from the text that the volcano had been dormant for more than 200 years. 7. Answers will vary but should include details such as: (Author's Purpose) *A Sleeping Beast*: to entertain or to give a fictional account of why the volcano erupted; *Fire and Ice*: to give facts and information about what Iceland is like and why it is called the Land of Fire and Ice; (Main Idea) *A Sleeping Beast*: An evil ruler who comes to

Iceland is stopped by an erupting volcano. *Fire and Ice*: Iceland is a land of extremes in which both fire and ice play a big part. 8. Answers will vary but should include that both passages tell about Iceland being a cold and icy place with volcanoes. "A Sleeping Beast" differs from "The Land of Fire and Ice" in that it offers a fictional account with Iceland as the setting, and "The Land of Fire and Ice" is informational text about Iceland.

Pages 15–16

1. A; 2. C; 3. C; 4. true; 5. nectar; 6. Greenville; 7. Answers will vary but should include that a colony is a group of bees that live together. 8. Answers will vary but should include some of the following details: *Honeybee Hive*: Bees live there. Bees make honey there. It is made of wax. *Same*: Different activities take place there, homes for living things, busy places, nurseries, and places for food; *Apartment Building*: People live there. It has a place to buy bread and flowers. It has a gym. 8. Answers will vary but should include a description of another busy, active home or environment, such as an anthill.

Pages 19–20

1. fiction; Answers will vary but should include that the poem is fiction because it describes events that did not really happen. 2. poetry, It has lines that rhyme. 3. nonfiction; Answers will vary but should include that the article gives facts and information about the topic. 4. Informational text; It provides information about a topic. 5. B; 6. A; 7. *A Box and a Can* (Kinds of Junk) old chewing gum, mismatched socks, broken chains; (Why is junk a problem?) It makes Benji's room messy. (What is the solution?) Benji must clean his room. *Space Junk* (Kinds of Junk) pieces of old satellites and rockets, bits of plastic, metal, glass; a tool bag; (Why is junk a

problem?) The junk can hit other satellites and rockets and can break space shuttle windows. (What is the solution?) No solution has been found yet but countries are working together to determine what to do. 8. Answers will vary but should include that both passages were about junk that needed to be cleaned up. 9. Answers will vary but should include that the poem is fiction and is about the junk in a boy's room, while the article is nonfiction and is about junk in space.

Pages 23–24

1. A; 2. C; 3. B; 4. D; 5. made maps, drew sketches, wrote reports, and took samples; 6. Answers will vary but should include that magma is hot and causes the water to boil, which results in an eruption. 7. *An Important Day*: Yellowstone was explored before it became a national park. The geyser was called Old Faithful because it was predictable. Hot springs were found in Yellowstone. The report from the expedition would be given to President Grant. *Geysers*: More geysers are in Yellowstone than in any other place on Earth. Old Faithful is the best known geyser there. It is easy to predict. It erupts about once each hour. It can reach 180 feet (55 m). Tourists like to see it erupt. 8. Answers will vary but should include a comparison of the information from each passage. Answers may include details that both passages described the eruption of Old Faithful, and both passages told how it got its name. Only "An Important Day" contained some historical details about Yellowstone National Park.

Pages 27–28

1. fiction; Answers will vary but should include that the story could not happen in real life. 2. fable; Answers will vary but should include that it is a story that teaches a lesson.
3. nonfiction; Answers will vary but should include that the passage

Answer Key

gives facts and information about the gold rush. 4. informational text; Answers will vary but should include that the passage provides facts and information about a topic. 5. a mighty steed; 6. true; The text indicates that the wife wanted the husband to buy a cow and sheep. false; The text indicates that some people who provided goods and services to the miners also got rich. 7. *One Golden Egg*: A. The goose laid a golden egg. B. The goose flew away. C. The farmer and his wife were poor again. *Gold Rush*: A. He found gold in the water. B. News about the gold got out. C. Fewer prospectors found gold. 8. Answers will vary but should include that in both passages, gold was valued and people felt they would become rich. Also in both passages, people were disappointed when that did not happen.

Pages 31–32
1. B; 2. C; 3. A; 4. Steam power was used for trains and in riverboats, as well as to make the railroad tracks that were needed. 5. John Henry was able to drive the steel spikes into the track and lay the heavy railroad ties. He could also break up the rock that stood in the way of the tracks. 6. Answers will vary but should include that "A Time of Great Change" tells that a steam drill could do the work of a dozen men using sledgehammers, so it would not be possible for a person to win the contest. 7. *John Henry and His Sledgehammer* (Main Idea) A man used his strength to help build the railroads. (Details) He was very strong at a young age. He used his strength while building the railroad. He challenged a steam drill and won. (Summary) John Henry used his strength building the railroad and won a contest with a steam drill. *A Time of Great Change* (Main Idea) The Industrial Revolution was a time of great change in the world. (Details) Machines, such as

the sewing machine, changed the way we made things. Travel changed with the invention of the steam engine. Communication changed with the use of steamboats and trains and with the invention of the telegraph. (Summary) The Industrial Revolution changed the way people made things, traveled, and communicated. 8. Answers will vary but should include that both passages tell about people who use their hands to do work. However, "A Time of Great Change" tells what happens after machines are introduced.

Pages 35–36
1. B; 2. D; 3. C; 4. D; 5. Steerage was the place just below the main deck of a ship where poorer passengers stayed. 6. The author means that the gift was perfect because the statue would be a symbol of freedom. 7. *What does it look like?* The statue is very tall and is a woman holding a torch. *Where is it?* It stands in New York Harbor. *Why did France give it to the United States?* The French people felt a bond with Americans and wanted to celebrate America's 100th birthday. *What does it symbolize for immigrants?* The statue symbolizes freedom and is a welcoming beacon to those who see her. 8. Answers will vary but should include that Bartholdi would likely feel very happy that Armando and his mother saw the statue and felt that she was holding out her torch for them.

Pages 39–40
1. D; 2. C; 3. B; 4. D; 5. garter snake; 6. alligator; 7. turkey; 8. *Facts:* Answers will vary but may include some of the following: Many presidents owned pets. The president and the president's family live in the White House. More than half of the homes in the United States have at least one pet. Some animal diseases can be spread to humans. In 2003, there was an outbreak of monkeypox.

Some states now ban wild animals as pets. *Opinions:* Answers will vary but may include some of the following: Some pets are typical. Pets such as snakes and alligators are unusual. Owning exotic animals is a worrisome trend. It is important to get the word out about the problem of owning exotic pets. Owning exotic pets is not cool. Wild animals should stay in the wild. 9. Answers will vary but should compare the author's purpose in writing each passage and include details from each passage to support the comparison.

Pages 43–44
1. B; 2. C; 3. global; 4. mapmaking; 5. maps on clay tablets, maps on silk fabric, maps on wooden boards; 6. Answers will vary but should include details that support the student's opinion. 7. Answers will vary but should include details that support the student's opinion. 8. *Maps from Long Ago*: Maps were tools that helped people find their way. People made maps on different kinds of materials. As travel increased, maps became more detailed. *GPS*: The military developed GPS. People use it to help them find their way. Satellites make GPS possible. (Same) Both help people find their way. 9. Answers will vary but should include details that show a general understanding of how GPS technology works.

Pages 47–48
1. A; 2. false, true; 3. Answers will vary but should include that the author wanted to support the main idea by giving examples of different kinds of animals that migrate. 4. Answers will vary but should include that the author wanted to support the main idea by giving examples of different reasons that people migrate. 5. not enough food to eat; 6. plentiful; 7. *On the Move* (Main Idea) People migrate for many different reasons. (Details) Answers will vary but may include religious freedom, better

Answer Key

opportunities, adventure, war, nature, to find food, or weather. *Animals That Migrate* (Main Idea) Animals migrate to survive. (Details) Answers will vary but may include that birds fly where it is warmer, African elephants look for food and water, caribou go to forests in winter, fruit bats search for ripe fruit, and humpback whales travel to warmer climates. 8. Answers will vary but must compare and contrast human and animal migration patterns.

Pages 51–52
1. D; 2. B; 3. C; 4. Leonardo da Vinci; 5. Orville and Wilbur Wright; 6. Orville and Wilbur Wright; 7. Leonardo da Vinci; 8. *Leonardo da Vinci* (Early Life) lived during the Renaissance, born in Italy in 1452, loved to draw and loved nature; (Major Accomplishments) painted the *Mona Lisa*, became interested in science and inventions; (Interesting Facts) did mirror writing, studied faces; was a man ahead of his time; *Orville and Wilbur Wright* (Early Life) lived in Dayton, Ohio, in the late 1800s; were interested in flying when they were young; made and sold kites; (Major Accomplishments) flew the first powered flying machine; (Interesting Facts) found ways to improve kites and bicycles; 9. Answers will vary but should include that all three had a curiosity about how things worked and shared an interest in flight.

Pages 55–56
1. D; 2. B; 3. A; 4. false, true; 5. natural events and people; 6. the homes or environments of the plants and animals; 7. *Keeping Balance*: made up of living and nonliving things; can be small or large; can be harmed by natural events and people; *Bringing Back the Wolves*: Herds can become out of balance. Imbalance can be caused by people. Both: Ecosystems must be kept in balance. Balance can be restored. 8. Answers will vary but should include a choice and details.

Pages 59–60
1. C; 2. A; 3. C; 4. D; 5. Answers will vary but should include that basic needs were food, shelter, and clothing. 6. anything people use to help them solve problems; 7. *Cool Animal Tools* (Key Details) Crows use pebbles to help them drink. Wasps use gravel, leaves, and sticks to hide their nests. Capuchin monkeys use stones to crack open nuts. (Main Idea) Animals use tools to help them solve problems. *Picking Up a Stone* (Key Details) Humans in the Early Stone Age first used stones as tools to get food. In the Middle Stone Age, humans began sharpening stones and using them to make spears. Late Stone Age humans began to use other materials to make tools. (Main Idea) During the Stone Age, early humans used tools to help them in their daily lives. 8. Answers will vary but should focus on the central idea of both passages.

Pages 63–64
1. B; 2. A; 3. C; 4. false, true; 5. The narwhal's tooth has a hard core but soft exterior, while the teeth of most animals are soft on the inside but hard on the outside. 6. difficult or challenging; 7. *The Top of the World* (1) extremely cold temperatures; little sunlight; thick ice sheets; (2) Inuits are a group of people there. Animals, such as the arctic fox, walrus, and snowy owls live there. (3) nothing; *Unicorns of the Sea* (1) icy waters; (2) Narwhals live there. They feed on shrimp, squid, and fish. Orcas and polar bears prey on narwhals. (3) Pollution and climate change threaten the narwhal's habitat. 8. Answers will vary but should reflect the student's understanding of the Arctic based on the passages.

Pages 67–68
1. fiction; The wind is speaking, which would not happen in the real world. 2. poetry, It has lines that rhyme. 3. fiction; It describes events that did not really happen. 4. realistic fiction;

The story is made up, but it is about realistic characters, settings, and events. 5. Answers will vary but should include that Nana was telling Henry to get ready to go. 6. Answers will vary but should include that the wind believes friendship is not possible. 7. Answers will vary but should include that the author included the detail to help readers understand that Nana was a fun person. 8. *Wind* (Character Traits) can do many things but cannot be seen; can cause fright during a storm; likes to be strong and cold; is unpredictable about where it will blow next. *Nana Ortiz* (Character Traits) likes to do unusual things; likes to spend time with her grandson; knows a lot about rock formations. *Henry Ortiz* (Character Traits) felt his grandmother was terrific; knows she is a bit unusual; was excited to see the rocks; felt the goblin trip was the best trip. 9. Answers will vary but should include details from each passage.

Pages 71–72
1. C; 2. D; 3. A; 4. C; 5. D; 6. true; 7. false; 8. *the King* (Why) He wanted to find the coins. *Pilar* (Did What) She gave nine coins to nine villagers. *Mom* (Did What) She asked Rudy to help pull weeds. *Rudy* (Why) He knew it was the right thing to do. 9. Answers will vary but should include details to show that the king was motivated by greed and getting more money, while Rudy was not motivated by greed, even though he wanted money for the video game. Students' opinions may vary about their favorite characters but should include reasons to support their opinions.

Pages 75–76
1. a jungle-type setting near a river where banana and mango trees grow; 2. the family room in a family's home; 3. Answers will vary but should include that the Baboon is an animal that wants other animals to think he is more important than they are.

Answer Key

4. Answers will vary but should include that Mom knows that Nicholas may sometimes frustrate Mason, so she tells Mason that because he is older, he has a responsibility to be more patient. 5. B; 6. D; 7. *Baboon* (Words) He said that Ant was so small that kicking her anthill was of no consequence. (Actions) Baboon helped Giraffe and the tiger cub. Baboon kicked Ant's anthill. (How did this character change?) Baboon stopped kicking Ant's anthill. *Mason* (Words) He told his mother that he would watch Nicholas. He said no when Mason asked him to play with him. He said, "Mom didn't say I had to play with you, just watch you." He said, "I'm sorry. That was an accident." He told Nicholas that he would help him get the blocks and build a tower with him. (Actions) He refused to play with Nicholas. He dropped his book and knocked over the tower. (How did this character change?) At first, Mason would not play with Nicholas. At the end of the story, he helped him pick up the blocks and said that he would play with him. 8. Answers will vary but should include that the main reason that Baboon changed was because Ant threatened to crawl inside his ear each time he napped unless he stopped kicking her anthill. Mason changed because he felt bad about knocking over the tower that Nicholas built.

Pages 79–80

1. realistic fiction; The story is about characters and a setting that could really exist. 2. science fiction; The story is about space travel and is about an event that could not really take place. 3. C; 4. D. 5. A; 6. B; 7. *The New Girl* (Beginning) Olivia looks around the cafeteria for a place to eat lunch. (Middle) Yasmin invites Olivia to sit with her and Lindsey. (End) The girls get to know each other and become friends. *From Planet Zeron* (Beginning) The spaceship lands, and the space family looks

out the window. (Middle) Father ChipChop explains that Rix needs to go to school while he and Mother ChipChop look for a place to live. (End) Caleb invites Rix to have lunch with him and they get to know each other and have fun. 8. Answers will vary but should include details that both passages are about being in a new place and that it is important when someone reaches out in a kind and friendly way.

Pages 83–84

1. fiction; The writer describes a made-up event. 2. poetry; The writing includes stanzas that rhyme; 3. fiction; The story is about a made-up character and event. 4. realistic fiction, Even though the story is made up, it has realistic characters and tells about an event that could happen. 5. Answers will vary but should include details such as a dance, a show, or a ballet. 6. The light show put on by the fireflies is a little like a fireworks show because both show bright lights at night, but the fireflies are from nature and fireworks are not. 7. Some examples include fireflies flashing; Hello, how; shimmering show; dazzling dizzy dance, fluorescent flings; crisscross; and fireflies flit; 8. Fireflies: Answers will vary but may include yellow twinkling light beams; bits of gold, shimmering show, dazzling dizzy dance, and starry ballet. The Light Show: Answers will vary but may include silvery light, pierced the darkness, thousands, blinked in unison, putting on a show, patterns, and flashed greetings. 9. Answers will vary but should include details that support the student's opinion.

Pages 87–88

1. a sewing shop in Philadelphia long ago; 2. a summer cooking camp; 3. a mouse; Answers will vary but should include that the mouse liked the shop because crumbs were there, and the mouse was happy to have witnessed history. 4. someone who is attending a cooking camp;

Answers will vary but should include that the journal writer is excited to be at camp and clearly loves cooking. 5. D; 6. A; 7. *Help, Please* (See) six-pointed stars; scraps of red, white, and blue; moonlight; and silvery needle; (Smell) fresh bread (Sound) clatter, scissors clicked and clacked (Touch) dropped my cheese, fine thread (Taste) fresh bread, and salty cheese; *My Cooking Journal* (See) big circle, tiny slits in the top, juicy red fruit, thin sheets of gingerbread, and fluffy white clouds (Smell) vanilla cake and blueberries, freshly mowed lawn; (Sound) berry explosions, campfire crackled and popped; (Touch) warm from the sun, fuzzy skin, and silky dough; (Taste) sweet juice, sprinkled with sugar, and world's best s'mores; 8. Answers will vary but should include details that support the student's opinion.

Pages 91–92

1. C; 2. D; 3. B; 4. A; 5. Emmett got the idea to make waffle cones when he got a whiff of Mr. Yosef's waffles baking in the next booth. 6. When Pablo saw the red yarn in the basket, he got the idea to use it to tie to the trees so that he could find his way back from Dr. Upton's. 7. *Ice Cream* (Problem) Emmett's family is running out of paper cups for the ice cream they are selling. (Solution) Emmett makes cones out of the waffles from the booth next door. *The City Blizzard* (Problem) Mother needs medicine, but the blizzard makes it too unsafe for Pablo to get it for her. (Solution) Pablo uses yarn to tie to trees to help him find his way back from Dr. Upton's. 8. In "Ice Cream," Emmett solved the problem. He made the decision to use waffles instead of paper cups to hold the ice cream. In "The City Blizzard," Pablo solved the problem. He made the decision not to tell Mother about the blizzard so that he could get the medicine she needed. Then, he made the decision to use the yarn to help him find his way.